Preaching & Intimacy

*Preparing the message
and the messenger*

Sermon Contributors

Tiffany Greer Hamilton is a recent graduate of Baptist Theological Seminary in Richmond, Virginia.

Sandra Hack Polaski is Assistant Professor of New Testament at Baptist Theological Seminary in Richmond, Virginia.

Charles E. Poole is pastor of Northminster Baptist Church in Jackson, Mississippi.

Beverly Zink-Sawyer is Assistant Professor of Homiletics and Liturgies at Union Theological Seminary in Richmond, Virginia.

Blythe Taylor is Associate Pastor of Wingate Baptist Church in Wingate, North Carolina.

Preaching and Intimacy
Preparing the Message *and* the Messenger

Charles B. Bugg

SMYTH&HELWYS
PUBLISHING INCORPORATED • MACON, GEORGIA
WWW.HELWYS.COM

Smyth & Helwys Publishing, Inc.
6316 Peake Road
Macon, Georgia 31210-3960
1-800-747-3016
©1999 by Smyth & Helwys Publishing
All rights reserved.
Printed in the United States of America.

Charles B. Bugg

The paper used in this publication meets the minimum requirements of
American National Standard for Information Sciences—Permanence of
Paper for Printed Library Materials.
ANSI Z39.48–1984. (alk. paper)

All biblical quotations are taken from the New Revised Standard Version
(NRSV) unless otherwise indicated.

Library of Congress Cataloging-in-Publication Data

Bugg, Charles B.
    Preaching and Intimacy: preparing the message and the messenger
    Charles B. Bugg
    p.   cm.
    1. Preaching I. Title.
    BV4211.2.B827   1999
    251—dc21   99-14807
                                                CIP

ISBN 1-57312-263-7

Contents

Contents

Foreword

In this lively, practical, and thoughtful book, Charles Bugg helps us reflect on the importance of intimacy in preaching. The author does not define intimacy in a technical way, but adopts a useful functional understanding of intimacy as quality of closeness in relationship. The presence of intimacy can help create a listening ethos in which a congregation is as fully present to the gospel of the living God as is possible in this world. Preacher, congregation, and God are together in a mutual bond of understanding. Within such a community the preacher and congregation can talk straightforwardly with one another and with God. The sense of joy is multiplied. The sense of power to bear one another's burdens is increased. The willingness to work together in mission is strengthened. Confrontation can take place in an atmosphere of mutual care. Intimacy shared throughout the congregation can become a part of the common life of the community. A sense of intimacy with the preacher, with other members, and with God can help the congregation be open to the full range of knowledge —from the most finely honed capacity for critical reflection to the deepest awareness of feelings in the pit of the stomach. Indeed, I have been in worship when an intimate moment in the sermon has become an experience of the gospel. The absence of intimacy can mute the most vivid imagery and the most potent ideas.

Of course, like every good gift, intimacy can be misused. A pastor can presume trust that does not exist. Preachers can reveal things in the pulpit about themselves or others that are distracting or embarrassing or that raise questions about the reliability of the preacher or even the gospel. In the name of intimacy I have heard preachers describe situations and relationships that have caused me to feel distant, distrustful, unclean, even violated. An intimate detail from the preacher's own life can cause the congregation to worry about the health or safety of the preacher to the extent that they lose sight of the gospel. I have heard preachers tell autobiographical stories whose effect is less to bring the congregation into the presence of the gospel than to call attention to some aspect of the preacher's life. Occasionally, I hear an intimate moment in a sermon that seems to be the preacher's cry for help. Nonetheless, when properly conceived and managed, intimacy can enhance the preaching moment for both pastor and congregation.

In this book Bugg draws on more than forty years of experience in the preaching ministry as student minister, local pastor, seminary professor, and guest preacher to help us identify qualities of intimacy that are appropriate to the gospel, that build up the church as a witnessing community, and that facilitate communication between preacher and congregation. He shows us many forms by which intimacy can come to life through preaching. The more obvious ones are telling stories with which the congregation can identify. Less obvious, but equally generative of closeness, can be moments of honesty when preachers struggle openly with the congregation with questions. Ironically, intimacy does not always mean being immediately within the world of another. Sometimes we need some distance from the other in order to see others in their distinctive otherness and to become aware of hidden and disrupting aspects of ourselves in relation to others and even to ourselves. But in a healthy rhythm of proximity and distance, intimacy can create the kind of close companionship in the body of Christ that empowers the minister as preacher, person, and servant of the gospel.

One of the permeating strengths of this volume is stories from the author's life and ministry. Avoiding dangers in the use of intimate material that I sketched above, Charles Bugg tells dozens of stories from his wide-ranging pastoral experience that illustrate how such material can help create the possibility for intimacy in the sermon. Some of these stories moved me to tears, others to chair-shaking laughter, others to poignant insight and recognition. "I've been there, too."

The book is organized into five chapters. The order of the chapters and their content reveal the serious theological approach taken to intimacy in this work. Chapter 1 focuses on intimacy with God. Bugg's God is clearly more than a cosmic therapist. God is the Transcendent Sovereign of the Bible, and of Luther and Calvin, whom we come to know through the incarnation. Indeed, at the heart of

Christian faith is the ultimate intimate knowledge: God is with us. The author leads us to recognize things that interfere with an intimate relationship with God: theological reductionism that shrinks our image of God, expecting too much of ourselves while not taking sufficient account of our finitude and not relying enough on divine grace, failing to pay enough attention to the living presence of God, taking ourselves too seriously and not letting humor make space for the awareness of the divine, not trusting God or one another.

In chapter 2 Bugg joins the shift in the contemporary homiletical movement towards the listeners by helping us think about how to develop intimacy with the congregation. The preacher needs to know the congregation and to speak in the sermon so that the congregation can recognize their questions, fears, struggles, and hopes. The preacher needs to learn to *listen* to the congregation—to its surface issues and to the concerns of the community that lie below the surface. Intimacy increases when the preacher comes into the pulpit with a message that is simple and clear. The congregation can understand the sermon and participate in it.

Chapter 3 deals with self-intimacy, with the preacher's knowledge of him/herself. We can speak honestly and insightfully to and for others only to the degree that we are honest and insightful of ourselves. This concern is not a justification for the navel-gazing and narcissism that are so prevalent in North America at the beginning of the new millennium. The author calls the preacher to the critical self-knowledge that is necessary to know who we are and what we can (and cannot) do before God. Towards this end, Bugg reminds us that we are *called* not only to preach, but also to know ourselves, even as we are known, as a resource for our preaching. Preachers need to have compassion, not only on others, but also on ourselves. In a provocative image Bugg reminds us that we preachers are both patients and physicians. Like the congregations to whom we preach, we *need* the hope that comes from the gospel. Of course, the gospel may prompt us to realize that genuine hope may come by way of repentance and struggle.

Preaching and Intimacy

According to chapter 4, the preacher can be intimate with the Bible. While Charles Bugg does not use this expression, his way of approaching the Bible is clearly to regard the sacred book as a Thou with whom we have a relationship. The Bible is more than a collection of propositions (though, to be sure, it contains propositions). It is a living story, a kind of biography of important chapters of God's relationship with the world. Because it is from another time and place, we need to honor the distance between the Bible and ourselves. However, if we maintain too much distance for too long, the Bible becomes to us like a quaint distant relative about whom we speak in hushed chuckles at the family reunion. Bugg urges the preacher to engage the Bible much like we engage a friend, honoring the integrity of the other while imaginatively entering into its world. Without collapsing the distance between us, we understand our questions about God and life refracted through its questions about God and life, our affirmations about God refracted through its affirmations about God. Reminiscent of Paul Minear, the author evocatively says that the Bible interprets us. As our mutual awareness increases, our intimacy increases.

Chapter 5 introduces the word "release" to replace the term "delivery" in referring to bringing the sermon to expression. "Delivery" sounds too much like the person who brings pizza to the door. For that person, the pizza is simply a thing to which the person is not intimately connected. The sermon, however, is a part of the self that is released into the life of the congregation. The preacher seeks a homiletical design that is consistent with the minister's personality and abilities, the characteristics of the biblical text, and the listening tendencies of the congregation. The preacher "speaks" the sermon (in contrast to reading it). Speaking creates a sense of immediacy and engagement. Bugg points out that some of us need help, however, at the point of "receiving ourselves," that is, accepting ourselves. We need to name and embrace our strengths, and our limitations. By getting the whole self inside the message, the preacher's whole self becomes a means of embodying the sermon. This increases intimacy in preaching because the congregation does not just consider an idea,

Foreword

or process an image, but encounters a message that is enfleshed. The encounter between preacher and congregation then becomes an event in which deep touches deep. In this context the listeners are friends who, even when they must hear (or say) something difficult, are still a community of support.

I am pleased to commend this book to seminary classes and to experienced preachers. Students will find it a welcome map to aspects of the preaching road that lies ahead. Veteran preachers will be reminded of qualities we have forgotten and will encounter some things that are fresh. In a world in which so many areas of life are impersonal, mechanized, even depersonalizing, this work on intimacy will help preaching become an occasion of encounter with a genuine other in the gospel.

—Ronald J. Allen
Professor of Preaching and New Testament
Christian Theological Seminary
Indianapolis, Indiana

Acknowledgments

"Acknowledgements" is not a word I like. Maybe it's because the word is too bulky, too long, or has too many syllables. I prefer the word "thanks." We all know its power. A parishioner says, "Thanks for being with me when I needed you." A student says, "Thanks for what you've taught me." A friend says, "Thanks for listening." When we receive words such as these, we may blush and say something like, "Oh, it was nothing." But inside we know it means everything. So I want to say "Thanks."

Thanks to the churches where I have preached and to the people who have listened to my stumbling words with grace. Thanks to my seminary, Baptist Theological Seminary at Richmond. Administration, faculty colleagues, staff—all make this a place where I wake up in the morning and look forward to going to work.

Thanks to Tiffany Hamilton, my teaching assistant and associate in our seminary's preaching center. Tiffany is one of those students who make teaching so enjoyable. She has made up for the computer deficiencies of her professor. Tiffany has that unique combination of attention to details while delighting in the fullness of God's creation. I will miss her greatly when she graduates.

Thanks to my family. My children, Laura Beth and David, have brought incredible joy to their father. With their permission, they have also provided an abundance of illustrations. I love them. My wife, Diane, and I are now embarked on our thirty-second year of marriage. As some of my friends remind me, I married "over my head." Yet, grace abounds. What a cherished gift Diane is. I couldn't love anyone more.

Finally, I want to thank the students who have allowed me to touch their lives and who have certainly touched mine. They have taught me so much by their commitment, their insights, and the sense of wonder they have when they find that they really can preach. Nothing is more satisfying for me than to see someone come alive to all that God has put within him or her. So I want to dedicate this book to my students—my teachers. I acknowledge you, but most of all I want to say, "Thanks!"

Preparing to Release the Message

It's been forty years since I preached my first sermon. I was fifteen years old. I had "walked the aisle" and told my pastor I felt called to the ministry. My pastor immediately put me to work. As I recall, my first sermon lasted eight minutes. The subject was faith. I took the concordance in my Bible, looked under the subject of faith, and my sermon consisted of everything I knew to say about almost every text I could find. The best that could be said about the sermon was, it was brief.

But the sermon was preached in my home church, the West Flager Park Baptist Church in Miami, Florida. You know home churches. With the notable exception of Jesus in Luke 4, almost every young minister finds a warm reception in his/her home place of faith. When I had finished my eight minutes of everything I knew to say about the subject of faith, I was greeted as a hero. Some people even said that I would be the next Billy Graham, probably the highest compliment a young minister could receive in 1958. That was heavy stuff for a fifteen-year-old. I didn't find out until later that every young minister at the time was being told by his home church that he was also the next Billy Graham.

I appreciated the encouragement, however. It gave me the confidence to hit the "sawdust trail" and to become a fiery youth evangelist calling everyone within earshot to a personal relationship with Jesus. As I look back to those years, I smile. What a sight I must have been. With my Bible open, my right index finger pointed, and my voice with the inflection of Billy Graham, I boldly pointed out sin and then proclaimed, "The Bible says. . . ."

One of these days I need to go back to those churches and do two things. First, I want to thank them for being so gracious to me. I have come to respect deeply the people in the pews. Let's face it. Those folks have to put up with a lot, and amazingly, they keep coming back for more. As I've grown older, I've become more grateful for the gift of attention that others have given to me. I know I was incredibly cocky as I went from place to place with my five sermons that so easily named sins and solutions. I had little sense of the complexity of life or how many people were struggling to make it from one moment to the next. In a word, I was naive. Yet, I remember the kindness with which people listened and responded. I need to thank those churches. They remind me that most people who hear our sermons are caring folks whose graciousness helps us preachers to keep on keeping on.

When I take the trip to those churches that listened to my fire and brimstone, I need to do something besides thank them. I need to apologize. I thought I knew too much about people and the preaching event. I was too hard on the listeners. I was too simplistic in the solutions I offered. While I tried to preach with what the old-timers called unction, I didn't preach with much understanding of who people were and even who God was. Few things are more potentially dangerous than lots of unction and little understanding. I was passionate, but I had little perspective on life. While I want to thank the people in churches who gave me the gift of hearing, I want to apologize because I was so busy speaking that I didn't give them the gift of my hearing. If unction without understanding is dangerous, speaking without first hearing is equally problematic for the preacher.

It's now forty years after those first stammering attempts to speak the Word. Interestingly, I'm still thanking people for their gift of listening. Of course, not everyone listens to me with rapt attention. Some nod off, and others look out the window probably dreaming of Sunday afternoon plans. But enough listen to convince me that proclamation still has a central place in the life of the church. I preach and I teach preaching not because I have run out of vocational options, but because I believe words are still a fundamental way God chooses to work.

That brings me to this book. No other person has affected me more in my ideas about preaching than Fred Craddock. I've heard many others say the same. When I first heard him speak, I was amazed at the aliveness of his preaching. Contrary to what Craddock claimed in the title of his first major book on preaching, he spoke to me as one with authority. In his second book, *Preaching*, Craddock introduced me to the term "intimacy" as it applied to homiletics. Intimacy was one of the six qualities Craddock noted as being essential in the

2

preaching event.[1] Rather than define intimacy, Craddock described it as the quality that helps to establish a relationship between the hearer and speaker. He also noted such things as eye contact in the delivery of the sermon and orality in the preparation of the sermon that help to facilitate intimacy.

I was hooked by the word "intimacy." I began to think about its multiple meanings for preaching. First, it affirmed for me the crucial role the messenger has in the message. The early church father Augustine wrote about sacred rhetoric. Borrowing from the thought of Greek rhetoricians such as Cicero and Aristotle, Augustine listed three essential components in communication: *logos*, *pathos*, and *ethos*. Basically, Augustine said *logos* is the appeal of a speech to the mind. Every message should have reason in it, a logic that gives cohesion and causes the listeners to say, "Now that makes sense."

At the same time Augustine was careful to say that sacred rhetoric should do more than speak to the mind. It should also address the emotions, which Augustine called *pathos*. Listeners should feel something. They should go away from listening to us saying, "Not only did I learn something and the message made sense, but also I was deeply moved by what was said." Augustine recognized early that people do not live by heart or head alone.

Logos is important. *Pathos* is important. Yet, Augustine said the most critical component in successful communication is what he labeled *ethos*. Ethos is the character of the speaker. People aren't just listening to a message; they are listening to someone speak the message. The "who" of the speaker affects people's listening more than "what" is being said.

This is not to diminish the importance of solid content in preaching. If nothing substantive is said, it doesn't matter who says it. A good person saying nothing was not Augustine's intent. As Henry Mitchell reminds us, we preachers come to the sacred desk "not because we have to say something but because we have something to say." What would we think if the following situation happened to us? We go to someone's house for dinner. The host invites us into a beautiful dining room. The best china and silver are on the table. Cloth napkins and an exquisite tablecloth greet us. "I'm sorry," the host says, "but we have no food unless you count the tomato juice and crackers you had when you first came." That's no meal! I'm going to stop at the first restaurant on the way home and say, "Skip the hors d'oeuvres. I want some food." Likewise, the importance of *ethos* doesn't mean we turn the preaching class into a finishing school where we polish the personalities of aspiring preachers but forget to remind them they are in business of feeding hungry people.

We need something to say, something that speaks to the heads and hearts of our hearers. Yet, it is "we" who speak. A sermon is not a sequence of words tossed casually toward a congregation. A sermon comes from the mouth of someone. At its best the sermon comes from the deepest places of the preacher's being, those places where we encounter God or struggle with God or wonder how God works to shape our lives and life around us.

I walk through the memories of those ministers who have spoken and shaped me. Most of the time I remember only the broad sketches of what they said. What I *do* recall is who they were. I remember a tall man, my home church pastor, who spoke with a monotone voice but who claimed our listening ears because he was a kind and loving pastor. I recall the pastor of the church I attended when I was in college. He was bright and articulate. He was warm and interspersed his sermons with humor and a smile that made the listeners laugh even when his stories weren't that funny. Something about the way that minister spoke the message caused me to feel close and connected to him. I was listening to preaching, but I was listening to a person preach. I like the word "intimacy" because, as Augustine reminded us, we don't listen to *logos* and *pathos* without also hearing *ethos*.

I am also drawn to the word "intimacy" because it suggests a more "holistic" approach to preaching. Frankly, one of the issues that has concerned me both as a teacher of preaching and a preacher is the issue of sermon delivery. I agree with Richard Ward that "delivery" is a misleading word. As Ward suggests, delivery brings to mind the person from the pizza place who arrives at my door with a product he's had no hand in preparing.[2] Delivery is a separate experience from preparation.

The same thing happens with a sermon. Hopefully, we're not delivering a product someone else has prepared. That's called plagiarism. Rather, the preparation of the message and the delivery of the sermon are so separated that often in the teaching of homiletics, we fail to help students see the connection between the work of the study and the witness in the sanctuary.

Instead of the word "delivery," I want to opt for the word "release."[3] What if we could teach the art of proclamation in such a way that people would see that what we are about isn't "getting up" a sermon but is "getting into" ourselves a message and then, "getting it out" in a way that draws people to listen. In effect, we release what we have received.

What I'm trying to do is to collapse some of the distance between the study and the sanctuary. I want to see the presentation of the sermon as an extension of the preparation of the sermon. I want to keep in front of those of us who are preachers that our task is both to prepare a good message and then to preach it effectively. From the outset of preparation, the preacher remembers that her ultimate objective is not to write a sermon that reads well but to prepare a message that will be heard. This approach demands careful attention to the oral qualities of the sermon itself and to the release of the words in a presentation that is authentic and appealing.

I recognize that to use a word like "appealing" sounds to some as if I'm capitulating to the folks who equate entertainment with worship. This is a legitimate caution. The primary purpose of the preacher is to try to speak words from God so that the Word of God can be heard. Those of us who preach are called to be faithful to that task. The place of worship is not the Sunday morning comedy club where we zing people with one-liners, water down the demands of the gospel, and count our success by the number of paying customers.

With that said, I still would make the issue that dullness and depth should not be synonyms for those of us who preach. After all, Jesus seemed to appeal to a lot of people through the way he spoke. "He speaks as one with authority," the crowd said after listening to the Sermon on the Mount. According to Matthew, those listeners went one step further. "He speaks as one with authority and not as our scribes." The best rendering of authority is freshness, first-handedness, a kind of authenticity that happens when someone is releasing a message that is alive in the person. "Jesus doesn't speak as our other teachers," the people said. "The message seems to come out of him. It's woven into the fabric of his life. Our other teachers cite authorities to support their messages. Jesus seems to have internalized the things about which he teaches. He speaks as an authentic witness to God, and we feel connected to him and his words."

Obviously, I have amplified the response of the crowd, but essentially this is what they were saying. The way Jesus gave a voice to the deepest things is appealing. He had something to say, and he said it effectively. Those of us who have been trained to be ministers know that much of our education was learning the skills to write well. We were taught to do research and to weave the results of that research into a fluid writing style. We were asked to think in terms of paragraphs and to know and utilize the esoteric words of our particular discipline. Phrases such as *sitz-im-leben* rolled off the pens, typewriters, and computers of budding theologians. Sometimes we seemed to delight in the obscure, which gave us a chance to fill up term papers and theses with footnotes that added length but little light.

Learning the skills of writing and how to put together a paper are, of course, valuable to us. Where would we be without rules of grammar? "*She and me* are going to the store." "This is a secret between *you and I*." These kinds of sentences grate on us whether we read them or hear them. Skills in writing and the use of language are important to all of us.

In much of our seminary education, however, we have emphasized writing skills to the unfortunate exclusion of speaking skills. While there is a positive correlation between the two, there are some significant differences. In preaching a sermon, a minister does not have the benefit of explanatory footnotes. If a preacher employs technical language, she has one chance to have it arrive at the ear. Complicated explanations of such things as the history of Philippi fall into the same category. The issue is not how much we know and can write about a particular subject, but rather how much people can receive.

This issue of "how much" affects the process of releasing the sermon. No doubt some sermons say too little, but the problem for many of us is that we want to say too much. We cram all the corners of the sermon with those wonderful "nuggets" that beg to be spoken. We dart up and down main roads, side roads, and the back roads of the text. Instead of the message being about one primary point, it becomes a hodgepodge of information with the minister mainly asking, "How can I get all this into one sermon?"

Not only does this create a problem on the hearing end, but it creates a real problem on the speaking end. How do we ever internalize something that has no organizing center or logical movements? No wonder some ministers keep their heads buried in the manuscript. Having too much to say is as much a pitfall in preaching as having too little to say.

Recently my wife and I took a trip through the mountains in North Carolina. I drove while she looked at the map. We finally reached our destination, but neither Diane nor I enjoyed the trip. I'm sure the mountains were beautiful. It was the spring of the year so I know the flowers and trees were gorgeous. I didn't have time to appreciate any of it, however. At every crossroads we looked at the map together to make sure we were taking the correct turn. The map dominated our trip. We were afraid of getting lost. We were uptight and tense. When we finally reached our destination, all we could say was, "Thank goodness, this is over."

When I finally reached the end of some sermons I've preached, I have said much the same thing. They were usually sermons where I knew I had a problem before I began. I was trying to say too much. I wasn't focused. I was anxious and uptight. I stayed glued to the map for fear if I made one wrong turn, the whole trip would be disastrous. There was no joy in the journey—only relief when I had finally finished.

During the last twenty or so years we have seen an increased emphasis on preaching in most seminaries and divinity schools. Part of this movement stems from the feedback of our graduates. Some of them are saying to their alma maters, "You taught me how to write.

You taught me language, theology, and church history, but you didn't teach me much about the practical areas. I'm in ministry now, and these people expect me to know how to put a sermon together. How do I preach?"

Those of us in theological education are foolish if we ignore this feedback or if we assume it's only the complaints of a few who really don't want the rigorous training of an academic education. As a minister who now travels to different churches, I hear this lament from some of our finest pastors. These are people who did well in seminary. They took the tough courses. The last thing they want is to reduce the seminary to simply a "how-to-do-it" school. For those ministers, it's not either theology or preaching. It's not either Greek or pastoral care. It's both/and. It's about finding the balance so that our graduates are equipped to think well, to love well, and to do well.

A second thing we need to do is to emphasize the power of words. I know there are plenty of jokes about preaching. "Don't preach to me! I don't need another sermon." Sometimes when I meet people and identify myself as a minister, I'm greeted with this benign look and some kind of comment like, "That's nice. My wife's grandfather was a preacher." The impression given is, we need people like you in the world for funerals and weddings, but if you were really on the ball, you would be doing something really important.

Not to be defensive, I want to shout, "I do something important." I speak about God; I try to address the deepest issues of people's lives; I want to be a change agent so that when people leave the house of worship, none of us is ever the same again. I will even tell people that I feel "called" to do this.

I feel called to preach. Somewhere in those places of our beings where our lives are really shaped, I feel "called." Can I describe call very well? Not really. Can I tell anyone else how he/she knows for certain that person is called? No. The fact is, I may be a fool—and to some, it may appear I am.

What can I say? Only that I believe I'm called, and on that I rest my case. I feel called to preach. What a joy it is to teach what I love. When I see a student become more confident, I feel so good. When I listen to the students encourage each other, I think I must have the best job in the world. When I have a student who says on the last day of class, "This class has helped me to see my call to preach," I respond, " You may be a fool. But welcome to the club. If it makes you feel better, I want you to know that the best thing I ever did was to join."

Notes

[1] The six qualities Fred Craddock mentions that should be sought in a sermon are: unity, memory, recognition, identification, anticipation and intimacy. See *Preaching* (Nashville: Abingdon Press, 1985) 153-69.

[2] Richard Ward, *Speaking from the Heart: Preaching with Passion* (Nashville: Abingdon, 1992).

[3] In a book on Christian education, Maria Harris uses the word "release." Harris says, "The final step in the creative, artistic process is letting go, releasing into the wider community the life which has been formed." See *Fashion Me a People: Curriculum in the Church* (Louisville: Westminster/John Knox Press, 1989).

Chapter 1

Connecting with God

I ended the introduction writing about "this call" to preach, so let's begin there. By the call, I don't mean so much a one-time experience in our lives when we encounter the irresistible urge from beyond to do nothing else than be a minister. For many of us, there was a time and a place in which we began to feel the stirring and made some response. For most of us, it had little resemblance to the drama of the apostle Paul's blinding summons to serve. Rather, that initial call came in quieter ways we interpreted to be the prompting of God.

I would prefer to see call as more than just a "once in time" kind of experience. Rather, I view it as the continuing presence of God who journeys with us and sustains us through the ups and downs of our ministries. At times the call seems more certain, and we go about our ministry with assurance. Other times the call seems less sure, and we feel alone and anxious. Nevertheless, we continue the journey because we have committed ourselves to the call by faith, and we know that faith and sight are not the same.

This image of call is important. Those of us who preach are pilgrims. We move toward the promised place. We are called to give a message of hope for the future. In the community of pilgrim people, we speak about the need for love and faith. Yet, we are always pilgrims. We know laughter and tears, success and failure, pleasure and pain. What distinguishes us as ministers isn't that we journey on a road separate from all the others. We do not travel some heavenly highway free from obstacles and detours. We are on the road, but on this road we are called to say that at times contrary to appearance, this road leads somewhere and that the unseen presence of God is guiding our steps.

Obviously, this call requires our own presence as ministers to God, and as we relate God's tender love to others, we are invited into our own relationship of that tender love. Without a sense of intimacy with God, both the journey and the speaking about its end and means become overwhelming. Despair is a vocational hazard for ministers. No wonder. Most of us have known painful times when duty required us to speak to the community about hope or love or faith and we had almost lost our own. We felt squeezed. When the preaching was over, we were beyond tired. We cried because we were talking about the way when we ourselves seemed to have lost our ways.

I'm not talking about the kind of intimacy in which I possess God and God "walks with me, and talks with me, and tells me I am his own." Perhaps it's the way I'm put together, but I've never been able to live with that kind of smiling assurance. Yet, I'm not willing to surrender the word intimacy or to speak about preaching as a craft that exists apart from God's calling. While I struggle with God's presence, like Jacob, I won't let go of this mysterious other until somehow I am changed. Preaching is not only about God, but also it comes from God. God is both subject and strength for our sermons.

In this chapter I will speak about some factors that often keep preachers from living in the presence of God and then relate some things that may help us to live into the Holy Other and to live out that Other's blessing.

The Tendency to Overanalyze

Theological education should help us to develop analytical skills. For example, we need to analyze the biblical text. What is its history? What was going on at Corinth that would cause Paul to write some of the things he did? What is the literary form of the text? Where does the text fit into the context? Why did Matthew begin his Gospel with a genealogy? Why does Matthew's family tree include several women, one being Rahab, known as "a woman of the streets"? How does each of the Gospels reflect the communities in which they were formed and fashioned? On we could go with all kinds of questions that are designed to help the preacher analyze and understand the text.

Exegesis is basically our asking questions of a biblical text. We want to get behind and underneath the words so we can appreciate better what they say and the way they are said. We even try to place ourselves into the lives of the first hearers of what later became the Bible so we can appreciate more the impact of what was said. If we understand the original languages, we analyze the Hebrew or Greek to see the nuances that are often missed in the English.

The study of theology is much the same. As ministers we try to analyze this God who reveals God's self, but understanding we always "see through a glass darkly." Nevertheless, we are called to speak to people about who God is and where God is. The pastor who walks into the hospital room where a child is critically ill instantly becomes the theologian to that family. "Do you think God is with us?" Mom and Dad ask. The parents are tired and worried. This is hardly the time for a lecture on the issue of theodicy. But in that moment when a family is struggling for faith in God, you as the minister, respond, "I believe God is here."

What gave rise to your credo? Somewhere in the process of thinking about God and analyzing the ways God works, you arrived at a truth that guides your care and conviction as a pastor. "I believe God is here in this hospital room," you gently say to parents who are afraid and to a child whose arms are bruised by tests and the tubes that run in and out of his body. Who knows? Your theology, or belief about God, may sustain this struggling family and may be the faith they need.

I am on the side of scholarly investigation. Some folks want to turn our educational institutions into little more than institutions of indoctrination. What a pity. We need ministers who have wrestled with tough issues and who have developed a faith that is their own. We need preachers who ask imaginative questions of a text and who come to the pulpit with more than superficial observations about what a passage of Scripture says.

But, while I'm affirming the need for scholarly investigation, I want to raise some concerns, particularly as they relate to preaching. What distinguishes preaching from other forms of communication is that our fundamental intent is to help God be made known in people's lives. As Christian preachers, our task is even more focused. We are called to proclaim the God most fully revealed in the person of Jesus Christ.

This means preaching is far more than simply good advice. Hopefully, we deal with issues that are critical to people. We speak about war and peace, abuse, ecology, racism, sexism, and a multitude of other issues that keep our world in discord. We talk about death and living, finding a life with purpose, experiencing God in our daily demands, and many other concerns that help people find joy in their own lives and in their relationships with others.

As ministers, however, we always come to these matters as people trying to bring a word from God. We want to represent a God who is big enough to help us put right what is wrong and to be at peace with what cannot be changed. We may and should feel deeply about those places in our world where ethnic differences, often fueled by religious hatred, are causing the death of far too many. Yet, we ministers need to remember we are not foreign policy wonks. We don't speak to social issues as government officials or to personal issues as advice columnists. As presumptuous as it sounds, we are called to try to speak a word for God and from God.

Obviously, this means our view of God is absolutely critical. Analysis in the art of theology is imperative, but this analysis can result in a kind of theological reductionism in which God becomes incarnated only in the categories we can understand and explain. The result is a diminishing of transcendence and the loss of a sense of awe and mystery by the minister. We preach what seems rational to us and dismiss what cannot be accommodated by our minds.

In some ways the whole postmodern movement has challenged our overreliance on rationality and our tendency toward reductionism. For one thing, the church has been confronted by people who have an intense spiritual hunger. About the time some of us ministers had declared the triumph of the secular and were trying to figure how we could keep the sacred alive on the margins, we discovered we had miscalculated. It's not that everyone is on the way to the church house on Sunday morning. Neither is everyone wanting to sign a card that says "Christian." Spirituality has become a broad tent, and the urge of people to find something more is finding countless expressions. The "great high priestess" seems to be Oprah Winfrey with her eclectic blend of positive thoughts and a belief in whatever you want to believe in as long as it makes you were happy.

At the same time we see the rush of folks to conservative churches where certainty is in no short order. Some of us have been standing on the sidelines critical of all of this "hoopla" in the name of Jesus or, in Oprah's case, "in the name of whatever makes you happy." I want to make a radical suggestion. Perhaps some of us less conservative ministers have lost out because we have not offered a God big enough for people's lives. Whittling God down to fit the contours of our minds may be no less a problem than the fundamentalist who whittles the size of Scripture to fit a box called inerrancy or infallibility. When we speak of the biblical God, we are speaking of mystery, explosiveness, intimacy, a God of reckless love and amazing grace. We are always talking about One who is beyond us. That recognition should not inhibit us in our preaching. Rather, it should give us courage as we preach about this God who cannot be limited to our likeness or be conformed to our mental graven images.

The pastor walks into the hospital room. The child is critically ill. Mom and Dad are struggling. "Is God with us?" They ask. "God is with us," the minister responds. Does the minister fully understand the meaning of having God with us? Hardly! Does the minister believe God is with them? Yes! God, we believe; help our unbelief. Intimacy and distance—we love God but don't posses God. It is that conviction that brings you and me to the hospital, to the sanctuary, and to all the places we go to speak about a God who is big enough for life.

Overexpectation of Ourselves

I often share with students in my preaching class that when I began my ministry, I had every intention of doing it all right. Other pastors before me had failed, but I would be perfect. That goal ended two weeks into my first pastorate. Christina and Bill Smith were among 75 members of Emmanuel Baptist Church, Rural Route 2, Lexington, Indiana. I was a seminary student. Each weekend my wife and I made the 40-mile drive from Louisville, Kentucky, to this church in the middle of the southern Indiana countryside.

Three things I noticed quickly about Bill and Christina. They were married, but they didn't sit together in church. I guess she liked it near the front, while Bill was anchored in the most distant pew. I also noticed that Bill was a farmer who wore his overalls to church. What stood out to me most of all was the expression on Bill's face as I preached. He glowered. I felt intimidated. I was a young preacher. I wanted everyone to like me.

On a Sunday afternoon I decided to make a pastoral visit to my unresponsive parishioner. I went to the Smith's old farmhouse, talked with Christina for a few minutes, and then she motioned me into the backroom. Bill was sitting in the hardback chair watching television. On the television was "Championship Wrestling." Bill hardly acknowledged me. I pulled up my own chair. Nothing was said. To put it mildly, Bill was engaged with the wrestling. I broke the silence with a classic line. I must have been tired, angry with Bill's lack of attention, or temporarily out of my mind. I looked at Bill, looked at the wrestling, and then proceeded to say, "You know that's not real."

The era of this perfect pastor had ended. Bill turned toward me. I fully expected anger. However, he was disappointed. His pastor had not taken seriously something he took very seriously. Christina and Bill kept attending church, but it took the rest of my five years at that church to recover my ministry with Bill.

I wish that was the first and last time I disappointed anyone. I think I have tried to be faithful to the task. I have wanted to say and do the right things, but I know there have been moments when I have passed by on the other side. Urban Holmes speaks about a potentially deadly combination that affects many ministers. It's the combination of high expectations and low self-esteem. I look back at my own ministry and see where these things have caused me enormous discouragement and even despair. I became a minister because I wanted to make a difference. I wanted my preaching to help effect change in people's lives. I wanted churches where I preached to become more of what I perceived the church needed to be and to do.

I had extremely high expectations of what I could do and what others should be doing.

At the same time I worried about how I was being received. Any negative criticism, especially about my preaching, sent me into an emotional tailspin. It was always my fault, so I needed to work even harder at preaching better. Whatever success I enjoyed was never enough. I see now that I didn't really enjoy any success I had. Either I felt I didn't deserve it, or I was concerned that if I did well, it only meant I had to do better the next time. Some of my friends who knew my struggle always loved to point out that Babe Ruth had more strike-outs than homeruns. That was supposed to make me feel better, but it never did. I just felt sorry for Babe Ruth.

I suppose if this were just my problem, I wouldn't write about it. However, when I have a chance to talk with ministers, and we move beyond the surface issues, I often find they deal with much the same thing. Sometimes I find this in my students. Most of them feel deeply called. They really want to make a difference. Yet, they are anxious and afraid. Who am I to help bring in the reign of God? Who am I to preach about being right with God when my own self seems so wrong? Good question.

When it comes to preaching, some of us try to camouflage our lack of confidence by giving the appearance we are in control. We have the answers. The pulpit becomes like the Delphi oracle. In fact, we may not even wait for people to ask questions. Since we have the answers, we will fashion our questions whether they connect with the listener's lives or not. This style of preaching is characterized by certain features. Usually the preacher assumes a different voice from the one we hear in private. He becomes more authoritarian and more dogmatic in the presentation. Instead of speaking as a pilgrim who is on the journey, this preacher may give the impression that she has arrived at the finish line of faith. The perspiration of struggle is replaced by a beautiful glow or by the angry scowl of someone who views himself as the parent and the rest of us as disobedient children.

It is important to remember that underneath this appearance there is a theological issue. If I feel I have to be someone other than who I really am when I enter the pulpit, what does this say about my own acceptance of the grace of God? What does it say about living into and out of myself as a unique creation of God? In a world that prizes authenticity, the demand for a preacher who sounds like the "stereotypical preacher" seems to be waning. Some people may feel more secure with the preacher who is bombastic, who scolds, who presents everything as if he operated with a red-letter edition of life, and who seems to have a corner on all there is to know about God. However, those of us who preach need to think about what this does both to our hearers and to ourselves. Among our listeners, it tends to create a passivity and fear in which God seems to be against us and always looking for the slightest mistake so God can pounce on us. This approach stresses judgment, but at the expense of the mercy and forgiveness of the one "who came to seek and save that which was lost."

Among those of us who preach, this approach to ministry deemphasizes our own dependence on God. We have to act like a minister, talk like a minister, live a minister, and we wind up creating an enormous distance between others and ourselves. When my daughter was planning her wedding, I recall a wonderful conversation we had. "Dad," she said, "I want you to walk me down the aisle and present me. After that, you can do your minister thing. But first, I want you to be my dad." So that Saturday afternoon, I was first and foremost Laura Beth's dad. I performed some of the ceremony, but my daughter said, "First, you are my dad."

I know the relationship with our children is special and different from others, but I was reminded of something important. For most of her life, I have been Laura Beth's pastor and preacher. My children never had much choice. When we moved to a new place, David and Laura Beth couldn't say, "I think we'll look around for a church we like." Dad was a pastor. Home and church home were givens. However, on the wedding day, the most important word for me was, "You're my dad."

I'm glad. I really am more than a minister. In fact, long before I was ordained, I was a human being and remain so to this day. What an awful burden to have to play the role of a minister all the time, especially when it causes us to be artificial and inauthentic. I don't mind being a minister. In fact, on most days I would not want to do anything else. I consider it to be a "high calling." I also know that many people expect a lot from their ministers. People look to ministers as role models, and it's sad when a minister runs off with the money, someone else's spouse, or does something else to bring discredit to the work of God. I get a little nervous around ministers who work too hard at "just being human." I have found I don't need to work at it; it comes naturally to me. I can be kind, but I can be hurtful. I can be generous, but I can be selfish. Laura Beth said, "I want you to be my dad." I thought back to the times when I was a good father. I listened, I supported, I encouraged, and I showed my love. Yet, I also remembered those moments as a younger minister when I was so busy trying to prove to myself and others that I could be a good minister. Sometimes I didn't listen or show love to my children. I am a minister. I am a part of the human family. It's both/and. It's for better/for worse.

Before I leave the issue of overexpecting, I want to mention another way that we ministers sometimes handle our response to preaching. The pulpit is demanding. At times we may camouflage our sense of inadequacy by appearing authoritarian and dogmatic. However, other ministers sidle into the pulpit with no confidence. They give the impression they do not belong, have nothing important to say, and are basically taking up everybody's time.

Humility is a virtue, but creating the impression that we are imposing on the listeners and will finish just as quickly as we can is not virtuous. Certain characteristics indicate this discomfort. For example, some of us may have a difficult time getting started in the release of the message. After thanking the choir, the music director, the instrumentalists, the sound technicians, and the custodian who turned on the lights in the sanctuary, the preacher is ready to begin the sermon. But not quite. "A funny thing happened to me on the way to the church today. Have you heard the one about the priest, the rabbi, and the Protestant minister who went fishing? It's really good to be with you this morning. I can't remember, but did I thank the organist for the offertory today? In fact, I don't thank Sara enough for her wonderful playing every Sunday, so let me just take a moment. . ." Are you tired yet? Where's the message? A few words of thanks are sufficient. All the rest indicates a preacher who is ill at ease.

One reason for this seeming discomfort may be that we have such unreasonable expectations of our performance in the pulpit that we hesitate to get to the sermon. So we play around to avoid speaking about the things of God. I often have students who say, "I'm afraid to preach." "Good," I respond, "You should be." "You don't understand. I'm really, really afraid to get up in front of others and speak to them about God." I say, "I think I do understand because I know that fear. Preaching is an awesome task."

Now, it's one thing if a person is immobilized by public speaking. That problem requires a gentle, caring approach. But with the normal fear of trying to speak the words of God into the lives of people, it means we, as preachers, need to remind ourselves of the most fundamental thing: we are dependent on God. As my preaching class moves toward the speaking of the sermon, I ask my students to visualize God beside them and underneath them. I want each of us to remember we are not alone. We speak about the very one who gives us the strength to speak about the very one.

In the 1800s the Danish philosopher Soren Kierkegaard influenced the view of preaching and worship when he called us to see God as the audience, the worshipers as the actors, and the proclaimer as the prompter. Kierkegaard's image reminds us that the church gathers to worship God, and the intent is not to entertain the congregants. Yet, I would like to see more emphasis on God not only as the one who receives our worship, but also as the one on whom we depend in worship. God is the subject *and* the source of our preaching and praise.

The Loss of Attention

Beneath all spiritual formation is the call to pay attention to God. Someone once said that prayer is paying attention with all of who we know ourselves to be to all of who we know God to be. It's being present to the God who is always present to us.

A number of years ago I heard a presentation on the components of a public worship service. The "invocation" was one of the topics. I grew up in a church where this prayer at the beginning of the worship service was used to "invoke" God's presence to us. The pastor or someone else would begin the prayer by describing how the people were gathered and then would plead for God to come among us. The image was of a God who was not with us. Therefore, God's presence had to be sought. Often, the person leading the prayer spoke about our sins and the need for this God to come to cleanse and to forgive us. Mistakenly or not, the impression I received was a God who was listening to our pleas and then deciding whether or not to come. The part about our sins made me think a major factor in the Divine's decision was whether we could become good enough or at least willing enough to be changed.

Frankly, I never could put all this together and figure out if God ever made an entrance into the worship service. Everything moved along as if God were there. We went through the same ritual each Sunday. We began by reminding God "where two or three are gathered . . ." After the reminder we told God we were sinful and unworthy, but we hoped that God would come anyway.

For a long time I thought of the public invocation this way. However, the person who made the presentation on worship opened my mind to a new way of thinking not only about the invocation but also about proclamation. The theological premise of the presentation was simple. God abides everywhere. God desires to become the sacred presence felt in everyone. The love of God is always reaching out in search of a recipient. Thus, the invocation is not a prayer in which we try to jar a reluctant God into paying attention or try to make God think we are willing to be good enough to earn the Divine's presence. Rather, the invocation is a call for the gathered people to be present to the God who is constantly present to us. We are not calling for God to love us if we are able to be better. Instead, we are calling for God to help us live and worship out of the joy that comes when we know the presence and love of the Heavenly Parent are unconditional.

How does this explanation of the invocation affect preaching? Well, it means that we adopt an attitude toward proclamation that is different from the way some of us have approached the pulpit. Throughout our preparation we aren't laboring to put together words that have to entice the Other to be among us. Neither do we speak as if we may be standing there alone with a group of people in front of us who are waiting to see if we can make God happen. Rather, we prepare and we preach knowing that God is with us. While we want to prepare the best we can, and while we want to develop the craft of preaching, we do not approach the process as if everything depends on us. Nothing saps the energy of even the most gifted preacher more quickly then seeing him/herself as the source of all words, the center of all change, and the engine for all energy in worship. No wonder some who preach live in quiet despair and either leave the ministry, stay anxious or angry, or surrender to a "ho-hum" style of preaching whose goal is just to make it through another Sunday.

Thus, it's vital to come to our calling with a sense that God is both for us and with us. If we believe this, the larger concern is remaining attentive to the presence of the One who dwells with us. Of course, the problem is not that those of us who preach decide one day we will no longer live with any awareness of God. It's not that we take a vote. There's no referendum to vote God out and vote ourselves in to go it alone. It's usually a gradual thing caused by at least three things.

First, we have to deal with the issue of busyness in our ministries. If we are parish ministers, we function like ecclesiastical general practitioners. We move back and forth among the multitude of expected and unexpected demands. We are with people, and then we are alone. Obviously, effective preachers try to structure the use of their time as much as possible. They guard those moments when they can be alone with the Alone, and they can focus the words they will proclaim to the people. Yet, even the most structured preacher knows that almost every day of ministry brings the unexpected call or the unanticipated concern. The problem we face is distraction. We move about the

22

myriad of tasks, and we begin to lose concentration and focus. People expect us to be there for them when they are hurting. Sensitive ministers, who usually make the best preachers precisely because of their sensitivity, feel most heavily the weight of other's expectations. The result is often a scattered approach to ministry that reduces effectiveness or triggers a rising anger and/or depression that reduces us to a perennial state of resentment.

A second factor that often blocks our attention to the presence of God is the distraction caused by our own unreasonable expectations. Let's face it. How does a faithful minister care for herself, her congregation, her family, and whatever else needs her care? In seminary I had a professor who told our preaching class we needed one hour of preparation for every minute we were in the pulpit. Since he was the professor and I was the student, I believed him. Think about this for a minute. When I left seminary, I went to a church that had a Sunday morning and a Sunday evening worship service. Plus, I did a Wednesday night devotional. I had a wife, a two-year-old daughter, and a child on the way. My congregation had a large number of older people, so I always had someone in the hospital. I also became hungry three times a day and didn't function very well without at least seven hours of sleep at night. You get the picture! Welcome to guilt city! If you have been able to make all of this balance, I hope you will contact me. I want to know how to do it.

Do you know what I tell my students? (It sounds almost heretical.) I tell them, "I know you want to paint the *Mona Lisa* of sermons every Sunday, but get over it. You don't have time to think every thought, do every word study, read every commentary, and produce each week a sermon that can be published in *Pulpit Digest.*" Those of us who preach always would like to do more with a sermon, but hopefully there is a life outside the study and sanctuary.

I don't say these things as a way to rationalize sloppiness in preparation or laziness in ministry. Frankly, some ministers lack the will or discipline needed for preaching. They come to the pulpit with a few stray stories and a text that sounds as if it is being read for the first time. People give us the gift of their presence at the time of -

proclamation. What a pity to have some preacher treat it so casually and to come to the time of preaching habitually unprepared. Yet, there is a sense in which we need to be content with the best we can do that particular week or that particular Sunday.

For the parish minister, some weeks are physically and spiritually draining. A child dies; a beloved member of the church passes away suddenly; the finance committee keeps you at a meeting for three hours arguing about the cost of new carpet for the adult building; your seventeen-year-old daughter announces that she's in love with the long-haired guy who has holes in all of his t-shirts and dungarees and who can't keep a job or stay in school; and you can add the next sentence. Talk about distraction, and some seminary professor adds to my guilt by making me think I need an hour of preparation for every minute of presentation. No wonder we ministers lose our interest in God. There's no grace here. It's all demand, and frankly, we get tired of feeling inadequate.

A final factor that blocks our attention to the presence of God is that God is the subject of our work, and sometimes we are present to the so-called holy so much that all we want to do is to get away from it. When I was a pastor, some people would come to the church house on Sunday and talk about how renewing worship was to them. I was glad, but sometimes I resented it. "All week long," they would say, "we are out there in the rat race of life, and then we come to church. We feel renewed." Do you know what I felt after preaching and leading worship on most Sundays? I felt tired. I wanted a nap. I would smile and shake hands at the back door, but by the time I reached our house, I was tired of being nice. "Don't talk to Dad," my children would say, "just let him eat lunch and take a nap." Blessed is the minister whose family understands and allows you to be human.

Of course, this whole thing is complicated by people who find out you are a minister and, therefore, assume that God and you are always bosom buddies. "So you're a minister," a young woman said at a place where I went to exercise. From the lilt in her voice, I could tell I had made a mistake in telling her my vocation. Sometimes I just tell people who have that "spiritual look" on their faces that I'm in humanities. I told this young woman, though, I was a minister. Do you know what it's like to have to give your opinion on the seven candlesticks in the book of Revelation while you are exercising on the stairmaster? Frankly, I don't have an opinion on the seven candlesticks, and even if I did, I don't have the energy to share it while I'm exercising. "I think my friend is about to marry the wrong man," she would say. "I know you're tired after working out, but what should I say?" The woman was wrong. I was beyond tired. I was rapidly moving beyond nice. But I'm a minister. I want to be nice. I didn't want to tell her to "bug off," so I said something. I don't even know what I said. I may have encouraged a marriage that should never have happened.

You know the story. As a pastor, I come to the church building. It's not a sanctuary for me. It's where I work, study, meet with staff and committees, and see people at their best and sometimes at their worst. I leave the church buildings, and often I'm still the "reverend" or the "pastor" or even "father" to some of my Catholic friends. I go to Rotary Club, and when the person who is supposed to do the invocation doesn't show, which is frequent, I'm the "designated pray-er." After all, God and I are bosom buddies. In a pretty profane world, like it or not, I'm the symbol of the sacred.

What if these people knew that sometimes I don't feel close to God? What if they knew that sometimes I don't even like the church I represent as a minister? What if people knew there are times I feel resentful, petty, pestered, trapped, discouraged, and downright angry? Why, if they knew these things, they would know who I sometimes am.

Sometimes this syndrome is called "compassion fatigue." As ministers we are called to care and to care often and to care intensely. While caring has wonderful rewards, it also has a cost. Few of us can keep caring at such an intense level without experiencing times when we feel drained and do not have the energy to care. Yet, Sunday comes with unrelenting regularity, and we stand and are expected to give a compassionate voice to the most meaningful matters.

In 1983, my son was diagnosed with a critical illness. For a year, the rest of our family watched as David suffered through radiation treatments and surgeries. The good news is that he made it through the darkness. While he still suffers some effects from what the doctors called a "pinealoma," our family is enormously grateful. What I remember, though, from that year when David was so sick is the enormous fear and fatigue we experienced. In fact, I recall going into the 8:30 worship service one Sunday morning and thinking, "I have no energy to preach." In some ways God seemed so distant. How could I call people to faith when my own faith seemed so fragile? The minister of music announced the first hymn. We began to sing,

> Great is Thy Faithfulness, O God our Father.
> There is no shadow of turning with Thee.
> Thou changest not, Thy compassions they fail not;
> As Thou hast been, Thou forever wilt be.
> . . . .
> Morning by morning new mercies I see.
> All I have needed Thy hand hath provided.
> Great is Thy faithfulness, O God, to me.

That wasn't a new song. I probably can't count the number of times I have sung those words. That Sunday, however, those familiar words became manna from heaven. I was tired; I was anxious; my faith in God was brittle. If preaching that day depended on my feelings, I could have the benediction and go home. Singing that song, though, was a searing reminder that proclamation, liturgy, whatever I do as a minister rests on a stronger foundation than who I am. It rests on God and God's faithfulness. That was the good news. I was in the worship service as a needy pilgrim, and that was alright. I didn't feel much like mouthing words, but how presumptuous of me to think that the worship service depended on my performance. In my chaotic, changing world I was singing about a God whose faithfulness changes not.

I talk too much about holy things. Maybe that is an occupational hazard. Sometimes I need to step back. A lot of times I need to be quiet and to listen. We ministers need to recover intimacy with God. Please hear me say, however, that I know from my own journey how easy it is to feel out of touch with the transcendent One even as we call people to be touched by this God.

Humor

Frankly, I am a little embarrassed to list humor as an antidote to serious concerns such as overexpectation and inattention. It sounds like telling a seriously ill person to go home, take two aspirins, and call the doctor in the morning. Humor does not sound like a potent prescription. Maybe that's because of the way I have often viewed humor. It's frivolous and distracting. It takes us away from the serious issues of life. Sometimes humor is inappropriate. It picks on people. Often, it's used to draw attention to itself. At the party we all dread the arrival of the clown who begins every sentence with, "Did you hear the one about . . .?" Notice we never get a chance to say, "Yes, I've heard." We hear whether we want to or not. I know humor has some bad press and deservedly so. Some preachers overuse humor perhaps as a way to try to make people like them or, even worse, to avoid some of the tough issues that are raised by the biblical text. Like almost everything with potential for good, humor can be abused.

Yet, one of the fundamental factors in spiritual formation is humor. Interestingly, in medieval physiology "humor" was viewed as one of four fluids in a person's body that determined such things as temperament and health. That philosophy carries over into our time. While our understanding of temperament and health have changed, we still use the word "humor" to refer to a bodily fluid.

Obviously, this is not a book on medieval physiology, and you already have everything I know. I want to talk about humor as an adaptive technique. Overexpectation is frequently born out of or at least nourished by the need to control. Some of us ministers marched out of divinity school and into our personal Zion. Well, it wasn't Zion yet, but we were determined to make people change and really become the people of God on mission. Our words would sensitize the saints, and they would all tithe, attend church, love one another, go to the homeless shelter, build Habitat houses, and be a bold witness to their semi-pagan neighbors.

The problem is I have never seen it happen that way. Maybe you have, and I'm glad. But I have found trying to change others and myself much more difficult. This is not an excuse to lower the bar on the proclamation of discipleship so that all of us can jump over it. Rather, it is to recognize that all of us resist change to some extent, and that we as ministers may need to adapt to what we cannot do or undo. Otherwise, we face the potential of some serious difficulties. Spiritually, we begin to lose connection to God. After all, God called us into ministry. Why doesn't God do something? Why doesn't God bring the kind of renewal in the churches we want to happen? Disillusionment with the Divine sets in. Intimacy is replaced by a perfunctory performance of duties or a kind of seething resentment that we didn't become the insurance agent our teacher in elementary school told us we would be good at doing.

This reality also affects our preaching. Some ministers start out in the pulpit with joy and enthusiasm. After a few years of little response, the passion is sucked out of their sermons. They come to the pulpit with the attitude, "This has to be done. Let's get it over with as quickly as possible." Other ministers allow their anger to be seen in the pulpit. They are harsh and judgmental. Every Sunday they came to the pulpit with the idea of working people over. How can I make them feel bad today? Our words became daggers that are designed to cut people and see how much we can make them bleed. There's a big difference between a scalpel in the hand of a skilled surgeon and a knife in the hand of an angry person.

By now, the positive effects of humor and laughter on the body are well documented. People write bestselling books in which they tell what laughing will do to improve the quantity and quality of our physical selves. Norman Cousins even wrote a book about his struggle with a life-threatening illness and how laughter was such good medicine. While I don't have the research other than the anecdotal variety, I want to suggest the value of humor for our spiritual selves.

I believe it makes good sense theologically. People who can laugh are usually folks who don't have to control everything. When I really laugh at something, I'm temporarily out of control. I go to see a movie with Jack Nicholson in it. All he has to do is raise his eyebrows and make one of his snide comments, and I'm gone. Or watching a Seinfield rerun, especially when it features Kramer. Kramer opens the door to Jerry's apartment, slides across the floor, and I'm gone. I know those things are silly, but I am a minister, and I deal with plenty of serious stuff. Frankly, I like something that is different, not too heavy, and will make me laugh. That is one reason I avoid movies that convey some heavy message. "It's a good movie," she said. "The ending will really make you think." That's all it takes for me to give it a thumb's down. I'm not going if I have to leave the theater and stay up half the night trying to decipher the hidden meaning.

But back to the real point. I know myself, and I think I have seen this same syndrome in other ministers. We tend to be serious people with a serious task. We like to stay in control, although we enter a vocation where there is much we cannot control. Walk into the average church. Look at the by-laws. Examine the committee structures. Stay there long enough to get a feel for those in the church who have the real power. Watch a church's business conference and the frenzied discussion about a cover for the communion table. I sat through that one. Those discussions usually come on the Sunday evening after you as the pastor have preached a passionate sermon about the church on mission. You wonder if anybody heard what you were trying to say. That night the big debate is not about missions but about an expensive table covering made with material from Madagascar. Don't laugh. I couldn't make something up that was this strange.

The next day I wanted to turn in my minister's union card. I wanted to cry, but then I started laughing. I wasn't laughing at the cost of material from Madagascar. I still think that's outrageous, although our church probably significantly improved the GNP of the country for that year. Nether was I laughing about the lack of impact my sermon had. I really thought I had redirected the route of the reign of God with that message. However, between Sunday morning and

Sunday night the vision had vanished. If we were going to do something for Madagascar, I would have preferred we sent a mission team.

What I was laughing about was the illusion that I somehow had everything under control and also the fact that the church through the centuries has managed to survive not only its enemies but also its friends. I had to adapt. The church where I was pastor was a good church filled with well-meaning folks. I didn't like the decision about the tablecloth, but that church had been around for a long time and had been generous and caring. It had managed to survive a number of pastors. Each time I went to my office I passed the pictures of all my predecessors. I wonder how many of them thought they had the church under control only to run into their equivalent of the Madagascar matter. Most of the ministers looked stern. A few of them were smiling. I have a hunch they were ones who finally realized that in the chaos we sometimes call church, God is in control.

It is funny to me that the church has survived its friends. Jesus' disciples hardly qualify for anybody's "Who's Who." In the book of Acts the church seems to make a good start, but it is not long until greed, lying, prejudice, and doctrinal disagreement interrupt the camelot of Pentecost. Corinth is hardly a place where I would like to be called as pastor. And what do you say to Ephesus where the congregation has forgotten its first love? Forget the persecution from enemies. It's a wonder the church has survived its friends. I guess it is a testimony to the guidance of God, and that God brings the church through overexpecting pastors and members who vote a sizeable chunk of change to cover the communion table with cloth from a country whose name I had trouble spelling.

Trust

If humor is part of our response to overexpectation, I'm convinced that trust is a critical component in combating inattention. Humor allows us to take God more seriously because we don't have to take ourselves so seriously. Therefore, humor helps us to adapt to those things we cannot control and frees us from the apathy or anger that often afflicts our ministry and our preaching when we find that not everybody jumps through our hoops. Trust functions in much the same way.

I have tried to retrace those times in my own ministry when I have been most inattentive to God. I recall the times I have shared with other ministers when life seemed to have lost focus for them. Several common denominators seem to emerge. Most of us take an activist approach toward our calling. We measure our success by what we do, and we usually operate with a "to do" list that is impossibly long. Personally speaking, I wish I could say that my work is motivated by a pure love for God. While I do love God, I also love the praises of people. I fear failure. I want people to like me and to like what I do. Probably my worst ministerial fear is to have a church tell me, "Chuck, you're not good enough. We need to find somebody who is better than you."

Since my "to do" list is impossibly long, I am good at telling myself that I'm not good enough. A Clinical Pastoral Education supervisor told me one day that I needed to bless myself more. It was right after a mid-semester evaluation. He had pointed out some good and some not-so-good things about my work in the hospital. I wanted more good before I left his office. "Is that it?" I said. "I have some more time. Say a few more nice things about me." My supervisor was a wise man. "You need to bless yourself," he said.

This man understood something about ministry and a great deal about me. I was at the front end of my vocational life. I would leave the seminary and the hospital and enter the church world. There would be some barbs and some boos about my work, but there would also be the blessing of kind and caring people. My problem was that I couldn't get enough blessings from others to feel blessed. "Your sermon was good," somebody said. Do you know what good is? Good is a "B." I wanted great! That's an "A+." Once in a while, an especially generous spirit would say, "That was a great sermon." That blessing stayed with me until I awoke from my Sunday afternoon nap. "Great!" Do you know what that means? What do I do next Sunday for an encore? What if that same person says "good sermon" the next

Sunday? To me, it meant I was slipping, and I was deathly afraid of that slippery slope of shoddy sermons.

Talk about confusion. Great was not good because that meant pressure for another great. Good was not good because it was not great. My supervisor said to bless myself. I was ashamed to tell him I didn't know how to let that happen. Not that I couldn't speak about the unconditional love of God or acceptance of ourselves as created by God. People told me they liked my sermons about the grace of God. Some folks told me they felt better about themselves after they listened to my sermons. What's that saying, "Physician, heal thyself." For whatever reason, I could prescribe for others but could not or would not let the medicine go down me.

The result was distraction. I was constantly pushed and pulled by my expectations. My answer to any perceived failure was to work harder. I turned in on myself more. In some ways it was a highly self-centered process. I worked harder, thought more about how I was doing, stayed tense and preoccupied, and paid less attention to my family and a whole lot less attention to God. My perception of God was a being very distant from me. And while I continued to preach on words such as "a very present help in time of trouble," they actually meant little to me. I lacked any real focus to the way I was doing life. I felt "unblessed."

Over the last few years I have begun to read the beginning of the Gospel of Matthew with new appreciation. For years I saw it as "just" a genealogy. I understood it was important to show the connection of Jesus to Abraham and David. The church had moved across the street from the synagogue, and while the preachers of the "Way" were proclaiming Jesus as the Messiah, they were concerned about staying connected to their Jewish roots. I also knew that Matthew's genealogy had a subversive quality to it. Not just men, but women were included in the lineage. In addition, some of the people had done things not unlike my discovering that my great-grandfather was basically a nice person but who didn't mind stealing horses on the side. I began to understand that a part of Matthew's intent was to say this is how God works—not always in the expected places and through the expected people, but this is the God who often seeks to write straight with crooked lines.

This new reading for me of Matthew's Gospel has helped to give interpretive shape to one of the most formative events in my life. My son's diagnosis with a brain tumor came just three months after I became pastor at First Baptist, Augusta, Georgia, and two months after my fortieth birthday. For me, becoming the pastor in Augusta was the culmination of a dream. It was and still is a big, beautiful, wonderful congregation filled with a rich history and great promise. When I arrived at First Baptist, the church had experienced some difficulties and had plateaued in its growth. I was determined that we would grow again, so I did what I usually do. I poured myself into the life of that congregation and worked as hard as I could to increase attendance, finances, and all the things that were tangible measures of success. In a way more potent than I even understood at the time, it was the only way I knew to feel blessed. Blessing was connected to success, which meant that my sense of worth was up and down. When things were down, I would work harder to get them up. When they were up, I worried about their going down. I don't recommend this as the way to live.

Suddenly, in the middle of this, my family and I were faced with the critical illness of our son. My way of doing life was also critically ill. I could not control what was going on in David's life. For certain, we sought the best medical care we could, but I now had a precious child who could not be made well by my working harder. Believe me, I went through a period when I bargained with God. I told God I would work even harder, preach better, love more, be a missionary to the interior of the Sudan, whatever. It became clearer as time moved along, however, that this was a situation that could not be resolved by greater effort and more doing. I also reached the outer limits of exhaustion and had no energy to do more.

David's illness also had the sobering impact of making me look at the priorities of my life. I was forty years old. What mattered most? I would have told you God and my family, but if you had looked at the way I lived, you would have concluded it was my work. I was still trying to get the blessing. Looking at David in the hospital bed one day, I felt an overwhelming sense of shame. How could I have gotten things so far out of the right sequence? In front of me was a son who loved me unconditionally, and I loved him with all of my heart. What a blessing! I had been so busy pursuing what I thought was blessing that I had missed the real blessing.

This is one of the reasons that the Gospel of Matthew has become a frame for me to try to picture some of the human journey. Do I believe God causes suffering? I cannot believe that. Rabbi Harold Kushner, in the extraordinary saga of his own son's suffering and death, deals with that issue. *When Bad Things Happen to Good People* is the story of a sensitive minister's desire to make at least some sense of random suffering. Theologically, Kushner concludes we are left to say two things about God: God is all-powerful and all-good. Kushner's conclusion is we cannot say both. He opts for the goodness of God. God cares for us and suffers with us, but God is not omnipotent. If God is all-powerful, then why doesn't God cure a child like Kushner's son? I think I know how Kushner feels. Walk down the hall of a children's hospital, look carefully at the suffering in some of the rooms, and then try to say glibly, "God is great; God is good."

Yet, that is precisely what I have chosen to say. It's a leap of trust. Otherwise, I am left with a God too small for my days and nights. This act of trust leaves unanswered questions. Why is there suffering, particularly among those who are so innocent? The best explanation I can give is the randomness that seems to be a part of our world, a randomness that brings grace to the seemingly undeserving and pain to those who appear to be pure in heart.

God is great; God is good. That is still the prayer our family says at supper every night. I say it because I believe it, and I want to believe it more. I trust God, but I want to trust more. I believe, but God help my unbelief.

I suppose we all define or describe trust in different ways. I have worked hard for the blessing. I have competed with all of my might for the prize. I have tried to direct the cruel winds of my child's suffering. In many ways I have attempted to shape life according to my bent. The result has been frustration and distraction. Pulled in many different directions, I have paid too much attention to the little and too little attention to the much. Working to help others find God for themselves, I have sometimes lost God for myself.

I want to do life differently; I want to live out of the power of that unseen presence. I want to love God more, and I want that love to be reflected in my preaching. In a word, I want to trust myself less and trust God more. Jesus said that some of us build our lives on shifting sands, but the wise folks build their lives on the solid rocks. I have built much of my vocation on the shifting sands. Even the house that some others may admire does not do well on the sands. I want to do life differently. My prayer is to be attentive to God, and to preach with a new focus. When the winds come and the storms blow, as they inevitably do, my prayer again is that I will live by trust in God, the God who is great, the God who is good.

Questions for Reflection

1. How would you describe your call to preach? Do you see calling as a "once in time" event or as more of a developing process?
2. What do you do to have fun? What makes you laugh? Do you utilize humor in your sermons? If so, why? If not, why not?
3. How do you respond to yourself when you don't preach as well as you believe you can? Are your expectations of yourself too high, or are they not high enough?

What Would Jesus Do?

Mark 8:27-38
Beverly Zink-Sawyer

The students in my preaching seminar were gathering for their Tuesday afternoon plenary session one day last semester. A doctor of ministry student in the class who serves a new church development in a growing suburb of Richmond always enjoyed regaling us with the latest antics of his postmodern congregation. That particular week it was the youth. A group of teenagers in the church had become swept up in the latest spiritual wave to wash over campuses. The content of their newfound spirituality consisted of an acronym and some new apparel. The acronym was "WWJD," and the new apparel was a sweatshirt bearing those cryptic letters. But the letters are not cryptic at all to those attuned to matters of faith. "What Would Jesus Do?" they ask. What would Jesus do if he were here, now, in my shoes, and yes, in the shoes of the curious who look at the letters and wonder what kind of new sorority they proclaim?

Not long after hearing my student's story in class, I opened an issue of *Time* magazine to an article about a growing number of religious groups on high school campuses. And there they were: a group of teenagers holding hands in a circle, heads bowed in prayer, all sporting identical navy blue sweatshirts with large white letters: "WWJD." Since then, WWJD apparel has become big business. Hallmark card stores are carrying a line of jewelry imprinted with WWJD; a priest in the Midwest is marketing his own line of WWJD clothes; even Cokesbury bookstore's last catalog had a two-page spread of WWJD wristbands and bookpacks and Bible covers. Just a few weeks ago, National Public Radio reported that the WWJD apparel craze is now a $3 billion business in the United States.

But something about this latest craze within Christianity troubles me. Each time I pass a rack of WWJD jewelry at the mall, which is happening more and more frequently, I get this gnawing uneasiness inside of me. What is it, I ask myself, that seems troubling about someone trying to behave like Jesus? After all, isn't that what we preachers spend our lives trying do—trying to encourage people to be like Jesus? Heaven knows the world could use a hefty dose of Jesus!

We need the grace of the one who would not allow the first stone of condemnation to be cast. We need the forgiveness of the one who prayed for his executioners as he hung on the cross. And yes, we even need the righteous anger of the one who threw the money-grubbers out of God's holiest place. In a world wracked by senseless violence, where children shoot other children on playgrounds, a world where nations are torn apart by ancient conflicts, a world where kindness and forgiveness are in short supply, people trying to behave like Jesus might offer us a desperately needed ray of hope. Heaven knows we need a world that follows the footsteps of Jesus.

But that's just the problem, isn't it? Which Jesus are we talking about when we try to determine what Jesus would do? That's really at the heart of what is so unsettling about Christians wearing sweatshirts and earrings emblazoned with "WWJD." Given the choice, we all want to do what Jesus would do—at least most of the time. The problem is, any attempt to put the essence of God made flesh in Jesus Christ into some formulaic rules, some template that can be imposed on any given situation—well, surely the wonder of the incarnation loses something in the translation.

My fear is that many who ask what Jesus would do if he stood in their shoes already think they know the answer. They think they know if Jesus would vote Democratic or Republican, whether he would be Presbyterian or Baptist or Methodist. They think they know what friends he would keep, what foods he would eat, and what causes he would champion. It's funny, isn't it? The Jesus most of us picture in our minds looks astonishingly like us.

I suspect God had a reason for sending Jesus before the dawn of the "Kodak moment." It's good that we have no actual pictures of Jesus. It's good because we have neither an image before which we might be tempted to bow down nor one that excludes those who do not look something like Christ himself. Still, we yearn to make Jesus in our own image. The Christmas song reminds us,

Some children see him lily white,
the baby Jesus born this night.
Some children see him soft and brown,
the Lord of Heaven to earth come down.

Mind you, there is something comforting in imagining a Jesus who looks like us. For a Jesus who looks like us gives us hope that somebody knows our troubles—and not just somebody, but Jesus the Christ. There is something comforting in picturing the Jesus who wept and laughed and ate and drank and was tempted in every way as we are. We look at the Gospel portrayals of Jesus and see there glimpses of our very human selves in the life of Jesus. And maybe, just maybe, we think, we have a chance at surviving this crazy life because Jesus walked this way before us.

What we fail to see, however, is that the real Jesus transcends our ability to define him. Even Peter, who walked and talked with Jesus, had to learn that difficult lesson. Peter wins the prize in Mark's Gospel for being the first to identify Jesus amidst all the speculation floating around. "You are the Messiah," he proclaimed with great confidence. You are the one on whom we're pinning all our hopes. But even Peter didn't get it. For the Messiah he saw was merely a reflection of his own expectations of grandeur—not the Messiah who would endure suffering and rejection and death on a cross before rising to new life. The real Jesus, Peter learned, keeps us guessing.

When we think we're being generous in giving away our shirt, Jesus says, we should give your coat, too. When we think we've been gracious by forgiving seven times, he says, oh no, forgive seventy times seven. When we think we've figured out how to save our lives, Jesus comes along and says we must lose our lives for his sake and for the sake of the gospel. The real Jesus works in surprising and unexpected ways—ways we can never anticipate, and rarely understand. He meets us in the most unexpected disguises. He challenges rather than confirms our assumptions. He leads us to places we would rather not go and calls us to do things we would prefer not to do.

In his book *Mere Christianity*, British author and theologian C. S. Lewis wrote about what it means to "put on Christ," to engage in a good kind of "pretending," as Lewis called it, about what it would be like to be the Son of God. "It is more like painting a portrait than like obeying a set of rules," Lewis concluded. "And the odd thing is that while in one way it is much harder than keeping rules, in another way it is far easier. The real Son of God is at your side. He is beginning to turn you into the same kind of thing as Himself."

What good news this is for all of us! It doesn't matter where we are when we encounter Jesus: rich or poor, wise or foolish, well-schooled or ignorant. We will all be transformed into something better through the grace of Jesus the Christ who, as we Presbyterians affirm after Communion, "makes us new and strong, and gives us life eternal"— all of us: the eminent theologian who thinks she has Jesus all figured out, the drug-addicted teenager who stumbles into a city church for shelter and finds there more than just a roof over his head, the harried single parent who is filled with self-doubt, and the corporate executive who is filled with self-importance.

No. We cannot even imagine what Jesus would do if he were here today, walking in our shoes. For the real Jesus, Jesus the Christ, is far greater than we can think or imagine. Maybe the best we can do is pray, in the words of the old spiritual, "Lord, I want to be like Jesus, in my heart." For only by keeping our hearts wide open do we have any hope of being transformed into something new by the grace of God— something, perhaps, far different from what we would expect. And if we happen, once in a while, to get it right—if we happen to do what Jesus would do—it is a gift of grace, not the calculated work of our own efforts. But neither do we need to fear the consequences if we sincerely try to be like Jesus and fail, for God's mercy is greater than our most grievous mistakes. May God grant us open hearts and willing spirits to follow the astounding, unpredictable way of Jesus the Christ. Amen.

Chapter 2

Dietrich Ritschl

Connecting with the Listeners

One of the classic debates among homileticians has been the role of the listeners in the preaching event. Specifically, the debate has focused on how much, if any, the preacher should take into account the listeners' needs and the way people hear.

Nobody is really saying the listeners should be completely overlooked. However, ministers heavily influenced by the preaching philosophy of Karl Barth's disciples, particularly Dietrich Ritschl, have criticized those who have been concerned about shaping sermons that are hearer-friendly. Ritschl and others warned that this could be overdone. In their opinion, we could wind up with a sermon that is entertaining but not really edifying. For theologians like Ritschl, the fundamental focus should be on the biblical text, and the sermon should explicate that text's meaning. If the sermon is heard, it will be the work of the Holy Spirit, not the efforts of some preacher who is preoccupied with the packaging of the message.

Those who disagree with this perspective usually emphasize two primary points. First, as we read the Bible, we discover very quickly that its writers and redactors sculpted it to be heard. The Bible is filled with devices that are designed to help communicate the message. Rather than being a flat book filled with propositions that ministers extract without any thought about how something is said, the Bible is alive with a multitude of forms. The Bible sings, shouts, whispers, tells stories, gives us history, and gives us hope. There is prose and poetry, proverbs and psalms. Like the Jew he was, Jesus seemed to relish the vehicle of a narrative. What is God like? Jesus does not answer with lengthy propositions about an unmoved mover or the first cause. *Yess!* What comes from the lips of the Rabbi are stories of a lost sheep, the lost coin, and the lost children. What emerges in these parables is a portrait of God who seeks the lost and gives parties when people are found.

The fact that the Bible seems to be crafted in ways that make its message more appealing reinforces the idea that contemporary preachers should also be attuned to forms of proclamation that connect to people. In a profound way, this makes both the encounter with a biblical text and the shaping of that encounter into the sermon a far more exciting enterprise. It helps us to see the far ranging topography of the Bible and to sing as we scale its mountains and to weep as we move through its valleys. Again, it keeps those of us who are ministers from a plodding approach to the preparation and proclamation of the sermon. If we view the Bible as all flat land, we usually view our task as preachers simply to excavate a chunk of earth and show it to the congregation in the same way every Sunday.

A second factor that has moved preaching away from the idea that the listeners should not be factored into the equation of proclamation is new attention to the way listeners receive and digest a message. Many communication teachers have highlighted the three obvious components of communication: speaker, message, and listener(s). Sometimes the impression is given that this event is a simple matter. The speaker decides what he will say. He shapes his focus into a form for communication. This is the message. That message is then received by the hearers just as the speaker presents it. The intent of the process is for the speaker to be clear in the presentation and for the listener to remember as much as possible of both the substance and sequence of the speech.

This model of preaching has much to commend it. If we as preachers are saying something important, obviously we want people to hear and retain what is said. It is also better for a speaker to be clear in what she says as opposed to being confusing and obtuse. Not many of us like to listen to someone speak who starts out not knowing where he is going and tries to take us with him.

This model is not entirely wrong, but it is too simplistic. For example, little attention is given to dressing an outline with rhetorical devices that will help the message to be remembered. The idea seems to be that if we can tell people what we are going to tell them, then tell them, and then conclude by telling them what we have told them, we will have accomplished communication. Perhaps, but maybe not. For example, much that has been written in the area of homiletics over the last twenty-five years has dealt with the power of stories. To me, the most fascinating part of this discussion has been, not the entertainment of stories or the ability of people to remember stories, but the potential stories have to change our lives. Stories can make us different in a way that information alone cannot.

Communication theorists point out that we live in plotted or story-like ways. For example, when I look back at my life, I remember I attended fourth grade at Fairlawn Elementary School in Miami, Florida. That is a piece of information. Because of overcrowding, we had our class in a portable room. More information. My teacher was Mr. Eardly, another piece of information. So far I have given you three pieces of information about me in fourth grade. You may conclude certain things from the information such as when I was nine-ten years old, I lived in the southern part of the United States (I realize some people in certain parts of the South do not claim Florida). You may also rightly deduce that we had a lot of children in our school that year since some of us were meeting in portable classrooms. However, those pieces of information really do not give you the whole story.

Mr. Eardly loved to teach. He was creative in his methods. One of the things we did that year was to recreate the solar system with papier-mâché replicas of the sun and the planets. We hung these from the ceiling of the portable classroom. That year I fell in love with the study of astronomy. Everyday when we walked into the classroom, we were greeted by the universe. Mr. Eardly was trying to get us to see the vastness of the universe in which we lived. Pluto was not just a planet with a funny name. It represented the far stretches of the world we knew at the time. As fourth graders we could hardly articulate the scope of what Mr. Eardly was trying to do for us. The fact is, however, since that time with a caring and creative teacher, the world has seemed much larger to me. While Mr. Eardly never talked about who created all of this, he helped me to see that God is always bigger than the stretches of my mind.

That is the story. A teacher, fourth grade, Miami, Florida, portable classroom—pieces of information. Only the story communicates how all of that information became transformative for my life. So we look at television today, and there are characters, locations, speech, movement, and all that goes with it. What makes all of these elements come alive is the way they are woven into the plotted story.

That is just one example of what communication theorists are reminding us. We live in an imaginative and sensory kind of world. Shall preaching stay focused on a string of propositions? We live in a more diverse world with gender differences, social differences, family differences, economic differences, and a multitude of other differences. Shall those of us who are male preachers and happen to like sports continue to depict life as everyone's being on the two-yard line, and it's always fourth and goal? Shall we continue to preach sermons about the family built on the assumption that most of our listeners are married and have two children? We live in a world where we recognize that people learn in different ways. Shall we continue to use the form of preaching that is most congenial to us and not diversify our presentation so that hopefully more may hear?

I am grateful to the homileticians who say to us as proclaimers that preaching must have solid content and that the Spirit of God enlivens the spoken word. They remind us that we have a story to tell, and that strategies for speaking the story must never take precedence over substance. These preachers also remind us of the transcendent dimension of preaching. Preaching is a craft, but it is never just a craft. Craft creates craftiness, and we as preachers spend too much time focusing on means to the message rather than the end.

Yet, our preaching is not spoken into a vacuum. It is spoken to persons. They come listening for a word. Some of them may not listen for long, but others will hang onto our words because they have nothing else on which to hang. As a preacher, I want to provide bread. I want to preach something with substance. If possible, I also want to do it in a way that makes the bread appealing. We come to listen . . . and to be fed. With this in mind, I want to speak about two fundamental issues with regard to hearers: What are people listening for and how are they listening?

Amen

What

Let me begin with the obvious. For anyone to presume that he or she can speak precisely about what everyone is listening for is presumptuous. It is worse than presumptuous. With all of the diversity around

44

us—with our increasing sensitivity to our differences—it is absolutely absurd to write as if I have cornered the market on what everyone needs. Yet, preaching and presumption share more than just their initial three letters. While those of us who are preachers approach our task, hopefully, with at least a modicum of modesty, we realize that to speak to the lives of people week after week is a presumptuous task. We interpret Scripture, and we interpret needs. Then we dare to try to bring those things together and even to claim in some way that we are spokespersons for God. That is preaching, but frankly, that is also presumptuous. With this caveat, I want to talk briefly about two categories of content for proclamation.

Immediate or Urgent

Every pastor, particular if she or he is in a pastoral context, knows what it is to preach in the face of some crisis. When I left the seminary to go to my first full-time church, I had been in the community about a month when a phone call came. A young man had been killed in a train/automobile accident. His parents lived near our church. This son was their only child. To make matters more complicated, he had recently been married. While the parents were not members of our church, they attended some, and we were the only church they had. I conducted the young man's funeral. Everywhere I went that week the tragedy was on the minds of people.

Naturally, I had left seminary with a six-month preaching plan. The plan never imagined the grief and shock that rippled through the community. The following Sunday morning I abandoned the plan and tried to speak to what we were all feeling. It did not take much intuition on my part to discern where the pain was. It was obvious to me, as it would have been to any other minister. That incident at the outset of my pastoral ministry, however, reminded me that sermons need to be connected to where people are, which sometimes requires real listening on the part of the minister. We listen to what people say, and we listen for what they do not say. We pay attention to their stories—what has blessed them and what has burned them.

Student
of life

45

We listen for the voice of the church—to the longtime member who remembers the pastor who baptized her and what that church family has meant to her through the years. We listen to the young couples who long for a church and a pastor who can help them and their children grow deeper in their understanding of what God wants them to be. We listen to the frustrated church member for whom nothing is ever right. We do not take all the complaints personally, but we are reminded despite our best efforts and energy that we cannot be all things to all people. We listen to the silence and to the whispers because the most important things many of us ever say get caught in our throats and barely dribble out of the corners of our mouths.

We listen, and then we preach. We give ear to life before we give voice to life. Otherwise, we wind up being noisy but without much really important to say. Most of us can listen through bad techniques in preaching. Those of us who preach know we have our own idiosyncrasies that others have to listen through as they hear us. However, I believe people will listen through those distractions if they know we have cared enough to pay attention to them and to speak to those things that are part of their lives.

In one of his books, the Jesuit writer John Powell says the deepest sin of the faithful is what he calls inattention. At times Jesus seems to suggest that the real opponent of faith is not doubt but distraction. Jesus calls his followers to "look," and they often stumble because they do not take the time to look beneath the surface at a lily, a bird, a Samaritan, or a child. The disciples are too busy anticipating what is ahead to see the value in what is around them. Consequently, they miss the power of the present.

We all remember people who paid attention to us and caused us to see the value in ourselves. On the other hand, few things are more painful than to be overlooked. I am convinced that listening is a discipline we can develop. By nature some folks may be better at offering the gift of their listening. However, all of us can work more at sharing this wonderful gift that brings such value to people when they feel they are being heard. Those of us who are activistic and who often say, "One day when things slow down, I'll smell the roses," can begin by recognizing that much of our churning is inside us. We need to be still on the inside because our feverish, frenetic lives are a reflection of our feverish, frenetic spirits.

Recently, I saw the gift of attention reflected beautifully. I was preaching a series of sermons at a church in Kentucky. This church has a ministry to a large number of deaf persons. Before the Sunday evening service, I walked into the sanctuary to greet them. What a warm group of folks they were. I knew that some of them could not hear me when I thanked them for their presence. Maybe they read my lips. I don't know. That part of the story is not nearly as important as what they did for me. As I shook their hands and said a few words to each of them, I saw faces that looked deeply into mine, and everything about them communicated they were present to me. I felt so valued and loved. Contrast that with a minister who greets you and me in the line after the service. "How are you?" he says, as he scans the rest of the people who are behind us in the line. I know what I am going to do. I'll say, "Fine," and drift through the rotunda and to my car. What I know, however, is that if I ever really need the gift of someone's presence, and I really need to be heard, I will not be back to see that minister.

Speaking to the needs of people grows out of our listening to them. Part of that presence is a product of discipline, but much of that flowers from the value we place on persons. I am convinced that this is a component of the whole preaching transaction that has received far too little attention. A preacher may be articulate; she may be trained to exegete a text; she may be able to craft an imaginative, intelligent message. But that message has to be spoken to persons. How we speak that message and the attitude we bring to proclamation are shaped significantly by our view of the hearers. Do we respect them? Do we speak to them as if we have all the knowledge, and they are sponges whose only purpose is to absorb what we say? Do we talk to them as if they are children, or do we see them as pilgrims with us in the journey? Frankly, some people are intimidated by the knowledge they think we ministers have, and we do little to bridge the distance between them and us if we appear arrogant.

Preaching and Intimacy

Recently, I preached at a church in our community that would be described culturally as a blue-collar congregation. Since the students in my classes fan out into all types of churches, I like the challenge of trying to communicate with many kinds of folks. The church in which I grew up was a mix of blue and white collar. While I considered both of my parents intelligent, the fact is that neither of them graduated from high school. I have been fortunate to get advanced degrees, but I have never felt removed from my roots.

I noticed that the man who was introducing me in the church talked more about the degrees I had and advanced training I had received. I was seated in the pulpit area so I could watch the congregation as all of this information was piled on them. Maybe it was partly my imagination, but it seemed to me the longer the introduction, the greater the distance grew between the hearers and me. I was glad to be there to preach. I spend most of my days interfacing with Ph.Ds or with students who have taken the introductory courses and love to talk about a "pericope" or the "*sitz-im-leben*" of a text. I like my colleagues and my students, but frankly, it is good for me to worship with others and to be reminded that everybody does not dwell in an "academic Zion."

So while I felt comfortable in this church, I really was not sure how comfortable they felt with me. I hope that by the benediction they at least understood I had not come there to try to impress them or much less to try to intimidate them with words or ideas that I may happen to know because my focus is theology. I am sure those people understood about other areas of life and could teach me so much. What I am talking is this: preaching is predicated on respect and care for people. Interestingly, we are told how Jesus saw people. He saw them as "sheep without a shepherd." What a beautiful portrait! Jesus did not see them as annoying people trying to take up his valuable time. They were not "interruptions" that kept him from doing more productive things such as getting ready for his next sermon. They were the hearers of his teaching and preaching, and Jesus saw their fundamental need to find something around which to center their lives.

I am not appealing for a kind of "syrupy" love for all humanity that disregards my feelings as a minister. I do get angry. I do get annoyed. Certain kinds of people can push buttons in me that make me want to get out of the room as quickly as possible. However, I am talking about a basic view of people that sees them as having intrinsic value because they, like me, with all of our annoying habits and insensitivities are children of God trying to claim our identities and value. That does affect the way we speak and helps to cut back on the temptation to use words as daggers or to talk to people as if they are beneath our own spiritual or intellectual level. I am a pilgrim among the people, and while my task as a minister is to try to guide people to the gracious God, I am not called to "tongue-lash" them into the kingdom.

In addition to the gift of our presence and respect, those of us who are ministers are called often to articulate the struggles of people rather than to provide easy, pat answers. This is particularly true with those urgent, immediate needs we face in the lives of others. When I was a pastor, I was called to the hospital one afternoon. A young wife and mother had been diagnosed with cancer. As the husband had shared the story on the phone, he told me the outlook was grim. She was given just a few months to live.

On my way to the hospital, I thought as I often have about what I would say to her. Should I tell her she might be healed? I so desperately wanted that, but I knew I couldn't promise that. When I walked into the room, she guided me in a way that was more beautiful than she knew. "I'm afraid. I don't want to die. I love my children and my husband," she said. "I am a Christian. My mother taught me about faith in God and how that faith abides with us. Pastor, I suppose I am living between what I feel and what I believe. In a strange way, I am afraid, and I am at rest." I said little because little needed to be said. She had articulated where she was and where most of us would be. There were no easy solutions to this situation. We live much of the time with a strange mixture of fear and faith, and sometimes one of those has the upper hand in our lives.

Preaching and Intimacy

In the midst of writing these words our family received word that our son David had another tumor in his brain that was growing and would have to be removed surgically. Several nights ago I was returning from a church where I had spoken at the ordination of one of our seminary's graduates. It was such a joyful time. The woman who was ordained had been my student in preaching class. I had watched her confidence in ministry blossom. I had seen her growing poise as she learned she could peach effectively. I had learned from the stalwart faith that had brought her to the seminary as a second career student. Now she was leaving our academic community, and she was going to fulfill her calling. I was filled with delight at having had a part in her ordination service.

But on my drive home I passed by the hospital where our son would have surgery. I suddenly became sick to my stomach. I remembered his other surgeries, the fear on his face as they took him to the operating room and the fear in our family's faces as we waited for some news. I recalled his pain, and how I wished above everything else I could bear that myself. We had ordained Mary to be a minister. She will be a caring spirit. Her deep faith in God will carry her through many things. I was happy and sad almost in the same instance. At her service I had preached about our need as ministers to persevere. A part of me wanted to give up as I looked at the hospital. Faith and fear—so close together.

If someone preaches to me, please do not offer me easy answers as if life always has symmetry and can always be interpreted. The fact is, life is asymmetrical, and we are staggered by the suffering some people face. Those of us who are ministers have been taught that we are to provide answers. We are the physicians of the soul, and we are called to diagnose and to prescribe. As much as I am drawn to Henri Nowen's wonderful image of the minister as the "wounded healer," I do not like the implication that we are always the "healer." Sometimes we are called to the proclamation of God's presence, not to the healing of all the pain people experience. We do not proclaim that presence easily. The Bible reverberates with the laments of people who thought God had deserted them. Even Jesus echoed the words of the psalmist,

"My God, my God, why have you forsaken me?" It is a prayer, but it is a painful prayer. It is a statement of faith, but it is a statement of forsakenness. In one sentence it captures the ambiguity of life.

We will preach to people who have been struck by the unexpected and who can barely make it to the church house. Their problems do not have easy answers. I couldn't put all the broken marriages together. I couldn't put all the broken lives together. Sometimes I can't put my own brokeness together. But we preach a God who is big enough to help us live the questions and to endure the seemingly senseless stretches of our lives.

Ongoing

When I teach preaching, I try to emphasize a holistic approach to the act of proclamation. For example, how a person speaks the word in the sanctuary is intimately connected with how he prepares the message. Those of us who have been educated in a script-oriented academic environment are tempted to prepare sermons replete with lots of conceptual material. That is the demand of most of the papers we are required to write. While I am not advocating that we eliminate good ideas in a sermon, I am suggesting that a sermon that is primarily a parade of concepts is very difficult for a preacher to visualize and is usually delivered in a ponderous, lecturing style. So as I teach, I am very interested in the sermon as a whole and seeing how all of the parts fit together.

Yet, in teaching I pull apart the components so that we can try to examine them more carefully. I am well aware that while I am talking the game of unity, I am often teaching in a way that dissects the sermon. I get some of this same feeling of contradiction when I speak about the needs of people as being either urgent or ongoing. Needs cannot be so clearly separated. A crisis in our lives may be the catalyst that causes us to face an ongoing struggle for meaning. If we face the illness of someone we love, how do we "face" that? What do we believe or not believe about God? What do we believe or not believe about the causes of suffering? Perhaps more importantly, do we believe that God works through the painful times of our lives to effect any purpose? So in the category of ongoing issues, I want to use one word but use it in two contexts. The word is "perspective."

First, at the heart of much of our proclamation is an attempt to offer people a new perspective on life. When Matthew announced Jesus' primary purpose in preaching, Matthew summed it up, "Repent, for the kingdom of heaven is near." In the preaching of Jesus, God was actively at work bringing a new vision to an old world. In fact, the vision is so cataclysmic that it can be described only by a word such as "kingdom" or "reign." Not everybody will be a part of God's new vision, however. While all are invited to be a part of this new reign, many will choose not to commit their lives to it. Those who do commit to this inbreaking kingdom must make a revolutionary decision. "Repent, " Jesus said. The call is to an absolutely new perspective on life. Repent is an incredibly strong word. We are not called to smooth out a few rough edges in our lives or to be a little kinder or a little gentler. Instead, we are called to see life as if God is in control and our lives are in the hands of a new monarch. In a word, this is a bold leap of faith that says the true reality of our living is found when we give ourselves unconditionally to the one who brings the news of the "kingdom of heaven."

This is the radical message we are called to preach. Interestingly, we seem to be living in a time when many people are more open to a new perspective and a new vision for life. As we move more deeply into what some have labeled the "postmodern" world, there seems to be a breakdown of what the sociologist Peter Berger has called our "plausibility structures." These are the beliefs we have used to make our lives more plausible and more understandable. The scaffolding upon which we have constructed our lives seems shaky, and there is a new openness to wonder and awe. This search for something beyond us that can give some sense to our existence takes a variety of forms. Check out a bookstore. The offerings in the section labeled "Spirituality" or "Religion" have dramatically increased in both number and the variety of solutions offered. While those of us in the Christian faith may disagree with some of what is being said, we should be grateful that more folks are searching for something. The hunger and thirst are themselves signs that in the church's proclamation, we have an enormous opportunity.

"Repent," Jesus said, "for the kingdom of heaven is at hand." Granted, we may have an argument about vocabulary. Words such as "repent" are not marketplace terms. They are not the vocabulary of the Junior League, the Rotary Club, or the college sorority. Those of us in the church will either have to try to bring these old words to new life, or we will have to choose a language with which people are familiar. Whatever choice we make on that issue, those us who proclaim to and for the church will have to recognize the need people have for something that is significant and substantive. Perhaps the reason many people have left mainline churches for other expressions of faith is because what we have offered from the pulpit has lacked passion, but most of all has not seemed all that plausible for the big issues people face. Offering people a new perspective is nothing less than proclaiming a whole new way to view our lives.

Recently at the thirtieth reunion of my college graduation class, I saw a woman whom I had not seen since graduation. I remember her being a stalwart in the Baptist Student Union. I was not as faithful as she was, but anytime I went, she was there. She went to church every week and was even a member of the Sunday School. That is nothing short of remarkable for even the most bonafide Baptist college student. At our college reunion she told me that twenty years before she had become a Buddhist. "How," I asked. "You seemed to be Baptist to the bone. You put the rest of us to shame with your commitment. While some of us were sleeping in on Sunday morning, you went to Sunday School!" She told me about the years after college. "I went on and did graduate work. Like many of us, I married, had children, and was involved in a demanding profession. However, something was missing from my life. I couldn't find it in church. I found it in the Buddhist faith." She then named it. What she had found was "peace."

I have studied just enough of the Greek language to know what I don't know, which is plenty. However, I do know the Greek word for "peace." I even know the Hebrew word. Most of all, I know as you do that it is an important word in the Bible. In fact, peace seems to be one of those things that are part of our lives when God is a part of us. Peace is important. Many of us spend a large portion of our lives searching for peace. We want to find an inner balance when everything around us may seem chaotic.

Peace seems to be an integral part of almost any Christian proclamation. Yet, my college friend had not found it in her tradition. She is a very bright woman. I would say that she had not listened well enough when the preacher was speaking about important issues like faith, hope, love and peace. Yet, I know what a sensitive person she is. I do not know this for sure, but I have a feeling that maybe some Christian minister who could have spoken to her about peace was too concerned about some matters that meant little if anything to the lives of the listeners. Perhaps no minister had preached about a God who was big enough for her life. Perhaps no minister had reminded her that the reign of God was breaking in, and that break demanded significant commitment. Perhaps, at the moment she needed it most, no Christian preacher had spoken about the new life in Christ and the peace that new life brings. All I know is, once she was a Baptist; now she is Buddhist. What she wanted, she told me, was peace.

Proclamation is the presentation of the radical call of Jesus to change us. That involves the inward journey. To follow the Christ is to see ourselves in a new way—to be given a different perspective. We understand that God loves us unconditionally. We see God present with us in our difficulties. To use the recurring image of the Gospels, we are in the boat and the storm comes. We never expected the storms. We realize they can overwhelm us. We are afraid. In our fear the one whom we follow comes to us. "Who is this?" we ask, even as the early churches asked in the midst of their own storms. Our response to that question is always a response of faith. Faith in the Christ gives us a different view of life. While the storms still come, we trust ourselves to the one who sometimes stills the storms but often stills us in the storms. Therefore, we preach the good news of a purpose and power in life found in a relationship to this God revealed most fully in Jesus the Christ.

The other side of proclamation is a new perspective on the world around us. To follow Jesus Christ is not only to receive but also to give. Repentance is turning to God to receive God's love; it is turning to God's world with a new compassion. Much debate within the Christian faith has occurred when one of these two elements is deemphasized or even excluded in the preaching of the church. For example, those of us in the evangelical tradition probably grew up with a heavy stress on coming to Jesus and the changes he would make in our lives. This evangelistic thrust in preaching was focused largely on individuals, and the call was for persons to profess their faith in Jesus Christ. The call of the church to compassion for the world was usually restricted to support and prayer for missionaries or to an encouragement for us to witness to other individuals and "lead" them to know Jesus Christ.

Other issues such as racial inequality, economic injustice, environmental concerns, or gender inequality were ignored or in some cases attacked because they would take the eyes of the church away from its primary task of evangelism. The suggestion was that if we came to Christ, all of these other problems would be rectified. However, the clear message was that bringing a person to Jesus Christ was much more important than trying to purify the drinking water of a community in the shadow of a nuclear power plant or trying to deal with the systemic issues of a society where the rich were getting richer and the poor were getting poorer.

In defense of this one-sided proclamation, it did create focus for the church, and it tended to instill passion in people for the work of evangelism. Those of us who grew up in this tradition thought we knew what the church was to do, and we did it with all of our might. We were single-minded in our desire "to win" people to Jesus Christ. The language of triumphalism was our working vocabulary. We were in battle. The enemy was identified as Satan. The Bible was our book, although I recall more preaching about the Bible than I do of the Bible itself. As Christians, we equipped ourselves with the armor of faith, and we set out to win the battle. We knew how to keep score. Each Sunday we counted the number of people who came to be baptized. Every week we knew if we were winning or if we had to redouble our efforts to achieve victory.

The social gospel was largely neglected except for times such as Thanksgiving and Christmas when we would gather baskets of food or bring toys for children who had no gifts. Even then we were concerned that the recipients of our goodwill would be presented with an invitation to know Jesus Christ, and there was no more joyous testimony than that of a church member who had delivered the gift of food to a person who had then received the gift of Jesus Christ.

While I recognize much that is neglected in this perspective, I am grateful for what it taught me about my own need for God. I was constantly reminded of my dependence upon God and that the source of deepest joy was a relationship with this God. While preachers spoke to me of God's judgment, they also helped me to understand God's grace and forgiveness. I was called to try to live a moral and ethical life, even though the definition of morals and ethics usually dealt with personal and private matters. Still I recall developing some sense of accountability about how I lived, what I did, and the potential impact on others. I learned that God was my God, but also the God of others. This was a God to be received as a part of us, but also to be shared generously with others. I learned that God is for us and not against us or certainly not neutral about us. These are beliefs I still cherish, and frankly, these are beliefs that mold much of my perspective about what needs to be preached.

In the years since my youth I have been shaped, not in discarding a personal need for this God whom Jesus revealed, but in enlarging my perspective about God's care for all humankind. In preaching, this has meant an expansion of my own perception of God's mission in the world. Wherever people are hurting, God is there and calls us to be with God's children. We are called not just to get people saved and on the way to heaven, but we are called to preach prophetically to those systemic problems that continue to oppress and burden God's children. We must ask ourselves and our congregations some very pointed and relevant questions:

- Can we be content with a system where some elderly are placed in institutions that dehumanize them?
- Can we continue to tolerate a health care delivery system that leaves many people without basic care?
- Should we be silent when our children are exposed to increasing levels of violence and decreasing family stability, and act out their pain in shooting their classmates and teachers?
- Does the right to bear arms really mean that we can create a society where those who are prone to violence are better armed than the police on our streets?

All of these issues and countless others involve God's children. Does God weep when those of us who have enough thank God for our blessings, but do nothing to extend the blessing?

Granted, we cannot mend all the broken pieces. No church can speak to all the issues. We only have so much time and energy to give. There is no virtue in spreading ourselves so thin that we say a lot about almost everything but wind up with no focus that gives us direction and strength to make changes. We are called to preach, "Repent, for the Kingdom of God is at hand." That is an enormously big challenge. Yet, as ministers in calling our churches to be the presence of God in the world, we need to remember that we do not have the resources to be everywhere doing everything. Not only is that exhausting, but it also can create surprising distance within our congregations toward some of these issues. The minister who inveighs against hunger, discrimination, and injustice does a noble thing. Following such a sermon, the congregation will probably vote overwhelming in favor of eliminating these things. The problem is, the sermon lacks "specificity," as Martin Luther King used to say. When we are called to be for good or against evil or even to bring in the reign of God, we will nod our heads in agreement, but it lacks a specific enough shape for us to respond meaningfully.

I have benefited greatly from the insights of David Buttrick. His most recent book, *Preaching in the Here and Now*, makes a strong case against the perception that the Kingdom of God is an individualistic experience where I spend my time singing solo, "He walks with me and talks with me." Buttrick is eager to recover a vibrant sense of the Kingdom where this community of faith thrusts itself boldly into the brokenness of the world. Who can disagree with Buttrick that the church is the church when it penetrates the world for which the Christ died?

What bothers me, however, is the deemphasis on the personal experience with God. Where will we continue to find the spiritual energy to make a difference in a not-always-receptive world if we cease to speak about our personal formation by the Spirit of God? Biblically speaking, a close relationship to God is not an act of isolation or distancing ourselves. Rather, it motivates us and moves us closer to do the work of God in the world. In a way, intimacy with God in spiritual formation creates a new intimacy or love for the world God has created and seeks to re-create. Individual piety that ends at the edges of our own selves is not only selfish, but also is a serious aberration of biblical faith.

How

How do we speak to people? If we are called as preachers to offer people a whole new perspective that revolutionizes life, what are some things we need to keep in mind as we speak the message? Obviously, valuable books have been written on the forms of a message or how to create a sermon. My intention is not to move down a road traveled much better and more extensively by others, but to offer two words that I believe need to guide our speaking the words.

Simple

Recently a spate of books have hit the bestseller list that are "how to" books for so-called "dummies." We can learn to operate computers, plant flowers, and do all kinds of other things. People do not seem to be insulted by the titles. When I decided to talk about the word "simple," I had this flash of people saying, "Now we have a book about preaching for dummies." Simple is not necessarily a complimentary word. I preached at a church where a woman said, "I don't understand much of what some preachers say, but I did understand you." Frankly, that comment ruined my afternoon. Maybe, I needed to be more profound. I do know a few multisyllabic words. Probably, I should have used those so the woman would have left church saying, "Now that was a seminary professor."

I am not using "simple" as a synonym for "dumb." Rather, I am using the word to try to address what I see as a growing phenomenon in our churches. When you and I speak as ministers, we hope to build on what our listeners already know. Increasingly we are speaking to folks who know less and less about the contours of faith and who have a relatively small working vocabulary when it comes to affairs of the spirit. This is not meant to be insulting to our hearers. A large part of the blame rests with those of us who have not been as intentional in our teaching and preaching ministries. The result is that the faith of some folks can be reduced to a cliché or a sound-byte.

[margin note: A WAY AROUND THIS is to offer Hooks Handles for people to wrestle & Reflect on & Around]

On my way to work one day I was passed by a car whose driver was going well over the speed limit. I did catch a glimpse of her bumper sticker. "God is an awesome God," it proclaimed. Apparently, this awesome God was not concerned about exceeding the speed limit. In fact, that is one reason I do not put any signs on my car identifying me as clergy or indicating any of my spiritual predilections. I have been known to blow my car horn on occasion, and I don't want to give a negative witness.

[margin note: — Simple Not Simplistic]

"God is an awesome God," the bumper sticker read, and I wondered what that meant. I have heard the word "awesome" used a lot lately as an adjective for God. There's even a spiritual chorus about "God is an awesome God." What did that mean to the woman whizzing by me on the interstate? Are we speaking about the God of creation or a God who had affected her life in some profound way? Had God helped her to restore a broken marriage or to get a meaningful job to which she was obviously late that morning? How would she explain "awesome God" to the mother of a child who had died or to the person who did not get a meaningful job? Maybe I am making too much of a bumper sticker. It is simple, but there is a kind of simplicity that is born out of ignorance of the real depth of biblical faith. In the place of any kind of significant biblical and theological perspective, we substitute bumper stickers and clever clichés and reduce complexity to an inane simplicity.

As preachers, we become people's theologians. That does not mean we need to weigh our listeners down with all the words we have learned in school and read in technical theological journals. Whether or not we use the word "theodicy," we are speaking to people who know that everything is not "sweetness and light." Unless they have opted to live in a unreal world where suffering is denied, our listeners understand that life is a mix of joy and pain, and sometimes the pain seems far more prevalent.

When I speak about simplicity in speaking the words, I am advocating a kind of preaching that recognizes many of those listening have few spiritual resources, and we have to preach those things that are foundational to our faith, basic tenets such as:

• Who is the God of the Bible?
• How does God reveal God's self?
• What does it mean to be a person of faith, hope, and love?
• What does the grace of God look like?
• What do we look and act like when we are grasped by the Gracious Other?
• Who is the church?
• What does the church do?
• Are we forgiven?
• How do we forgive?

On and on we all could go with those things we call the fundamentals but that often have been assumed and ignored in our preaching.

People will fill the vacuum in their lives with a bumper sticker spirituality or with a library of thin volumes written by beauty queens or ballplayers. It's fine if these people give their testimonies. However, I do not want Miss America or the Most Valuable Player of the National Football League shaping my theology any more than I want someone who loves heads but has never been to medical school performing neurosurgery on my son. I know the bumper stickers will always be with us. I know there will be church signs that will read, "If life gives you lemons, make lemonade." I know there will be the Miss or Mr. Whatever who will tell us that if we just trust Jesus, we can look like her or him. Some of that will always be present. However, the opportunity is there for preachers to speak with a profound simplicity to the questions all of us ask.

Clear

Simplicity and clarity are intertwined. We seldom find one without the other. Clarity is facilitated by attention to oral factors such as tight sentences, active verbs, and appropriate pace in speech. However, I want to emphasize two things I often find in my own preaching and in the preaching of my students. The first is the attempt to say too much in the sermon. Put positively, as preachers, we need to know what is the point of our sermons and to use material that enforces that point. Tom Long calls this the "focus" of the sermon. Before we begin to create the sermon, we decide what we want to create. That objective then becomes the magnet around which appropriate stories and other materials cluster. Otherwise, we wind up with a sermon that is out of focus, and we all know how hard it is to look at or to listen to something that is blurred.

Interestingly, trying to say too much in a message usually stems from the fear of the preacher that he or she will have too little to say. Consequently, we load up our sermons with all kinds of information, illustrations, and insights. For the listeners, the problem is not that there are not good things being said. The difficulty is that it is too overwhelming. We want the band to play one song at a time. If the sections in the band all decide to play something different, we will stop listening or excuse ourselves at the first break because we are overwhelmed.

Another factor that contributes to the lack of clarity is the failure of some of us preachers to understand the power of repetition. African-American proclaimers have utilized this rhetorical device most effectively. However, those of us in the white tradition of preaching have felt that if we say something once, people have heard it and grasped it. This gives rise to a type of preaching that is a parade of propositions that marches by the ears of the listeners in relentless procession.

We need to keep in mind that many of the folks who come to our churches already live in a frantic, cluttered way. They come to church out of breath from lives that are too busy and too burdened. If we speak to them about too much, it will be more than many of them can bear or hear. Also, if we speak too ambiguously because we ourselves are unclear about the point of the sermon, it will be difficult for our listeners to comprehend.

As I am writing these words, I am in the surgical waiting room with my wife as our son undergoes surgery to remove his tumor. Writing for me is a kind of therapy. As I am trying to write, however, a woman nearby is carrying on a ceaseless, one-sided conversation. I know it is not nice to overhear somebody else's conversation, but her voice carries throughout the room, so I am not really overhearing. This woman's husband is having surgery. Her friend, the listener, is waiting with her. I know we all handle our anxiety differently. This woman talks incessantly, moving from one subject to another with no transitions that I can tell. I have heard about her love for animals and the fact that her son wants a girlfriend. She has spoken about Carolyn, Tom, Mike, and somebody who "scowls" a lot. Already, I have come to a deep appreciation for her friend who quietly listens to a stream of information that is giving me a headache. I cannot help but think about my preaching. Preaching still makes me anxious. I wonder if anyone leaves the sanctuary when I preach saying, "I have a headache."

In addition to knowing what the point of our sermon is, we as preachers also need to know what our purpose is. What are we calling people to do or to become? Augustine said a sermon should "move" us. What are we calling people to move from or move to in their lives? If preaching is persuasive, as I believe it is, what are we trying to persuade our listeners to do? Some sermons call us to be "more

Christian." Some call us to be "more committed." Again, no one will disagree. The problem is that we do not know how to actualize those things. The call to specific action or specific change is missing.

I recognize that some sermons need to have a more generic intent or purpose. Some messages are designed to encourage a church family. Some churches, like persons, lose confidence in themselves. These churches have moved through conflict or may have had a minister who abused their trust. Like ourselves at times, about all they can do is exist. They doubt they have anything to offer. Any sense of mission is clouded by confused feelings and wondering how God can use their pain for some purpose. At those times we who preach need to be gentle and simply to remind them and ourselves of God's provision.

Comfort is a Big Theme

Often we ministers miss the mark by calling the church to faith in general but not to places and people where care and compassion can be given. We may talk about the care of the church for one another, but fail to offer a specific intergenerational ministry where the church can break out of its age divisions, and unity can be born out of diversity. One of the most meaningful experiences I remember as a pastor was when our children's choirs and our senior adult choir joined in a common presentation. Not only was the cantata beautiful, but also the caring shared between the two generations was inspiring. Like many churches, our educational staff was structured on an age-group basis. Unfortunately, this structure tended to segment the church, and our staff had to be intentional about ways to coalesce the congregation.

I am convinced today that people want to commit themselves to something meaningful. Charitable agencies in our communities do not mind asking people to give their time, energy, and money to specific projects and ministries. Why should the church do less? Why whittle down our demands so that people can join our churches and do nothing? When I give my life to something, I want to make my life count, and I want to make a difference. This may be the day in preaching when we need to recover the challenge and to remind our listeners that to follow Jesus is a call to an intimate relationship and a costly obedience.

Questions for Reflection

1. Imagine the people to whom you preach. What are some of the spiritual needs in their lives that need to be addressed?

2. What social or communal issues need to be addressed in your community? If you had the opportunity to speak for fifteen minutes to the people in your community who exercise the most power to effect change, what would you say to them as a minister?

3. Think about the people to whom you preach. How do they hear? Recall the things they remember as they leave the church. What do they recall after a month? What and how did you communicate those things?

And Yet

Psalm 66:1-12
Charles E. Poole

Several years ago I read about an interesting church in Arizona. It was a congregation of high-church Presbyterians who were not comfortable with a lot of spontaneous "Amens!" and "Hallelujahs" during worship, yet they wanted to be able to express their joy and praise in some unscripted, albeit subtle, way. They finally settled on a solution to their dilemma. The ushers handed out helium-filled balloons to all the worshipers each Sunday. Then, during the worship service, if someone felt a particularly strong urge to say, "Hallelujah!" or "Praise the Lord," they simply let go of their balloon, and it would meander on up into the rafters, a silent sign of high joy and deep praise.

That old article came back to me when I read this week's psalm. If the one who wrote Psalm 66 was an Arizona Presbyterian, he would have been sending up balloons by the bunches! Such high praise! Such boundless joy! Such wide-eyed wonder at the goodness and greatness of God:

> Make a joyful noise to God, . . . sing the glory of his name; give to him glorious praise. Say to God, "How awesome are your deeds! . . . All the earth worships you. . . .

The writer of Psalm 66 is a passionate leader of congregational praise. He is awed and amazed by the goodness of God, and he is urging his companions to join him in joyful praise. The Psalmist is floating balloons to the glory of God, and he invites the congregation to join the celebration.

But the Psalmist's life has not been all celebration. He has also seen more than his share of trouble, sorrow, difficulty, and pain. The Psalmist has obviously been around the block a time or two, and it has apparently been a rough ride. About midway through his poem of praise, the Psalmist turns his voice from the people to whom he has been singing and addresses his song to God. There is a key change from major to minor, and in a softer, slower voice, the Psalmist sings to God:

You, O God, have tested us; you have tried us as silver is tried. You brought us into the net; you laid burdens on our backs; you let people ride over our heads; we went through fire and through water.

The Psalmist recites in his songs a long litany of terrible troubles. It is reasonable to assume that this is a postexilic psalm, a song sung after the end of the Babylonian exile, a poem that recalls the complexity, difficulty, and sorrows of being uprooted, displaced, and bereaved. The Psalmist says, "God you have let some awful trials come our way. We've been trapped, trampled, and troubled. We have been through fire and water." It is quite a recital of pain and trouble that the Psalmist sings in softer voice and minor key. but then, when the story has hit rock-bottom, when the song has reached its depths, the tune takes a turn. The tune turns on the hinge of that little single-syllable, quarter-note word, "yet." Psalm 66:11 reads, "We went through fire and through water, yet you have brought us out to a spacious place." After rehearsing all the pain and sorrow, the Psalmist takes the song in another direction. He says,

And yet, you have brought us out of all that trouble and into a spacious place. Despite the despair of the past, you have kept us moving and seen us through. We thought we would never make it, and yet, here we are. Life was pressing down and closing in, and yet you brought us out into a spacious place.

The notion of "a spacious place" may well ring a faint bell of memory. This is not the only place in Scripture where the idea of "a spacious place" is cited. In Job 36 there is a sentence that reads, "[God] allured you out of distress into a broad place where there was no constraint." In Psalm 18 we read, "In the day of my calamity, . . . the Lord was my support. He brought me out into a broad place. . . . my feet did not slip." Then, in Psalm 31 we find these words: "I will rejoice and exult in your steadfast love, because you have . . . taken heed of my adversities, . . . you have set my feet in a broad place." And this in Psalm 118: "Out of my distress I called on the Lord; the Lord answered me and set me in a broad place."

This "spacious place" we encounter in today's psalm is a recurring image in the Hebrew scriptures, and it always appears in sharp juxtaposition to distress, trouble, and danger. To be in a "spacious place," or a "wide" or "broad" place means to be in a place of quiet and healing and recovery. In these Old Testament passages, a "wide, broad, spacious place" is the opposite of trouble, danger, and difficulty. The Psalmist says,

We were going through such a hard time. Our lives were in such disarray. We were in the fire and the flood, trapped, trampled, and torn asunder. And yet, God enabled us to live through it. We thought it would never end when we were in the middle of it, and yet God brought us out into a wide place, a place where we could breathe again and laugh again and live again. If someone had told us we were going to have to bear all that burden and face all that pain, we would have sworn we could not live through it. And yet, here we are. We were squeezed on all sides by the toughest, hardest, narrowest narrows of trouble, and yet God has somehow brought us back out into the light and put us into a wide, open, spacious place.

That is the song of the Psalmist. Little wonder that when the Bible was translated into the Latin Vulgate, this psalm, Psalm 66, was given the subtitle, "Psalm of the Resurrection." Little wonder. This Psalm sings about God enabling us to live into, through, and beyond the worst that life can bring, and then bringing us out of life's darkest shadows and tightest narrows into the light of a new day and the rest of a wide open place. It seems to have the ring of resurrection hope buried alive inside its words of sorrow and celebration.

It rings true on our ears, too, because many of us have, somewhere along the way, lived through something that, if someone had told us we were going to have to live through, we would have sworn we could not do it. And yet, here we are, alive, in a spacious place. God does somehow enable us to stay on our feet and keep moving. The terrible time does pass. And by God's grace, we live to be glad again; we come out of the dark narrows into a wide, livable place. But we are never quite the same. When, finally, we do come out into a large place, we carry inside us the lingering memory, and the lingering effect, of the narrow darkness. We are not the same, or if we are the same, we are of all people most wasteful.

In his book, *The Morning After Death*, L. D. Johnson quotes that wonderful old line, "Only pagans waste their pains." Indeed, it is so. There is no waste so profligate as the waste of our pains. To have been through the hard narrows of fire and water, and then to come out into a wide place without having gained new sensitivities, compassion, and depth is to waste the very pain that could have changed us for better forever.

Once, while browsing the shelves of a bookstore in Washington, D.C., I happened across a book cover that stopped me in my tracks. There, in huge block letters was the one-word title:

PAIN

Down below, in tiny type, crouching inside a pair of parentheses was the subtitle:

(The gift nobody wants.)

Indeed, pain is the gift nobody wants. And if we waste it, it isn't a gift. It can be a curse that hardens and diminishes us. But if we refuse to waste our pain, if we choose to let it be a surgical gift that opens us up to God and out to others, then, ah, then the results can be a sight to behold: We see with a softer eye; we speak with a quieter voice; we understand with a kinder heart; we care for others with a more open hand.

Ernest Hemingway, in a letter to F. Scott Fitzgerald, once wrote, "If you've got the pain, use it." If we have the pain, we can use it. We can let it be a gift—an awful gift, a gift we never would have sought, a gift we hope never to see again, but a gift nonetheless—a gift because we let the pain of life color, soften, and open our eyes to see other people and our own lives through the clarifying lens of our own pain. Irony of ironies, being squeezed down by the hard narrows widens our lives and makes us larger of spirit and greater of heart.

These things I do not say easily or lightly or with the naiveté of unbruised optimism. This is not syrupy-sweet optimism; this is the depth of realism: Life will press us down, not because God means it to be that way, not even because God is "testing us." (I can't quite fit that view of God inside the glimpse of God we find in Jesus.) No, life will press us down just because life is that way. Life can squeeze us down into hard, tight, narrow, sad places from which we just know we will never be delivered. Life can squeeze us down into such hard places, and life will. We will stumble and stagger beneath awful loads. We will. *And yet*, it is God's nature to somehow see us through.

At times our lives will be depleted by complex problems and heavy burdens that rob our sleep and close our throats, *and yet*, we live to laugh again and sing again and let go of balloons in wide places again. Sometimes the heart does break—I mean it really does break to the point that you just know life is never going to be simple or happy or good again—and yet, God keeps you on your feet. God gives you enough strength to do the next thing and, by the grace of God, you emerge from the narrow darkness with a wider heart and a deeper spirit.

Life has sometimes been so hard that we were sure we would not make it, and yet, here we are. Sometimes I wish God would do more. Sometimes I wish God would step in more and heal more and fix more and just do more. And yet, the truth is, God has done a lot. God has done so wonderfully and so much, or else, we wouldn't be here, would we? Amen.

Chapter 3

Connecting with Ourselves

When I lived in Charlotte, North Carolina, I bought most of my clothes at a certain men's store. I was usually helped by a young man who worked there. He was good with helping me to get clothes that fit, and I figured I needed all the help I could get. Whenever I bought a suit, the salesman and I would go through the same routine. He would remind me that one of my shoulders was lower, one of my legs was longer, and as he was marking the suit to be tailored, he would tell me about other things that needed to be done to make the suit fit well.

I never pretended to have perfect body symmetry. However, I always thought my body shape was fairly normal. But by the time this young man had finished putting all those white marks on the suit, I felt embarrassed to be seen in public. I wondered if everybody else was looking at my lower shoulder and longer leg. The salesman assured me he wasn't trying to make me self-conscious. He just wanted to make certain that the suit fit me. I guess that is what I really wanted because I kept going back. "It probably hurts you when I tell you these things," he said, " but remember my job is not just to get you to buy a suit, but to buy a suit that fits you."

I have been guilty at times of teaching preaching as if "one size fits all." Those of us who are preachers have certain things we become enamored with, and we tend to promote those things as critical to proclamation. Sometimes it's the form or the shape of the sermon. For awhile stories were the only way to do sermons. While outstanding homileticians cautioned against the abuse of stories, some of us did not pay close enough attention to their warnings. Some ministers simply strung together unrelated stories and called that a sermon. People in the congregation walked away saying, "What was that all about?"

On the exegetical side of the preaching event, some ministers became fascinated with the "hermeneutics of suspicion." Every text was approached with an eye to its deeper, hidden meaning. Any familiar interpretation was discarded because, for the suspiciously oriented proclaimer, "familiarity bred contempt." Imagine the surprise of our listeners. Some of them thought they knew the Bible. However, our job as preachers was to subvert their "sub-texts" and to help our hearers understand that they really knew nothing unless they put on the eyes of a liberationist, a feminist, or a womanist reader. This approach was an overcorrective measure. While it called attention to important issues, it took the Bible out of the hands of the middle-class couple in Peoria who were trying to find the peace of God in the problems they were facing.

These are only two examples of what we preachers sometimes do. Very valid forms for preaching or new hermeneutical approaches are offered, and instead of making them a part of our homiletical repertoire, we make them normative. We can give our listeners the impression that there is a certain, or "right," way to exegete biblical texts, to structure sermons, even to communicate the message. While those of us who teach preaching may voice support for the diversity of our students, we do not always honor that diversity by celebrating the variety of gifts we encounter. In a profound sense, one size does not fit all when it comes to the preaching event.

Therefore, in this chapter I will focus on the proclaimer. Again, a sermon is more than a sequence of words floating through the air hoping to arrive at the ears of listeners. Those words come from the lips of a preacher, but more importantly, those words come from the life of a preacher. Three elements are a part of the preacher and inevitably affect the words s/he speaks.

The Call

Many of us can point to a time in our lives when we felt a special sense of call. For some people, the call to a special kind of ministry was dramatic. Like Paul on the Damascus Road, these ministers experienced something that forever altered their lives. They need no other corroboration of their call. Something special happened, and there has been no doubt. For these ministers, the call was an epiphany.

For others of us, the calling was less intense. We use words such as "impression" or "feeling" to speak about the moment in our histories when we somehow sensed the prompting of the Holy One. We may even employ the categories of psychology to help interpret what happened. Maybe we were trying to please mother or father. Some of us were the "good" children, and we heard the voices of Sunday school teachers and others whom we respected, "You certainly would make a good minister!" We were eager to please God, the church, our parents, or the adults we respected. These factors became a part of our call.

I most relate to those who began their journey toward ministry on the basis of a whisper. In fact, I have often used the word "impression" to describe the initial stirrings I had. While sometimes I have wished for a more dramatic testimony, I heard no voice of God or no sound of cherubim or seraphim saying, "and who will go for us?" As a fifteen-year-old, I had a feeling I should preach, and I believed that some of my gifts matched the call. So without all the fanfare that Isaiah experienced in the Temple or Saul encountered on the road, I said softly, "Here I am, send me."

Later, as I looked back, I saw some of the social-psychological factors that undoubtedly contributed to my call. I did want to please my parents. I did want to be accepted by the church, and what better way than to be their "preacher boy." While I was shy in some ways, I did like the attention that came when I was speaking to people. I felt I had some facility for public speaking. If all of our motives for doing whatever we do have to be absolutely selfless, then I need to confess my failing. I took the road called ministry for a variety of reasons.

At times in my life I have felt apologetic about this. What a wonderful thing it would be to talk about a clear call with uncluttered motives. Wouldn't it be better to have one of those absolutely defining moments when you and I crossed over the river to the vocation of ministry and never looked back? Maybe, in some ways, it would be. Imagine how dramatic the testimony would sound. "I was a drug pusher. I worked for the mob. I was an alcoholic who lost my job and family, and I was sleeping under railroad trestles at night. But then Jesus came to me in a shining light, told me to follow him, and I've never turned back." I have heard stories like that and experienced goosebumps all over my body.

In contrast, imagine how my testimony sounds. I was fifteen years old. I was basically a good child. I liked to please people. One day I felt "impressed" to be a preacher. That's it—just an impression. In looking back, I see now how my need to please probably had something to do with my call. I also liked the positive feedback people gave me when I spoke. While I was concerned that people heard about the God who loves them in Jesus Christ, I was also concerned that the hearers liked me.

Granted, this is hardly a "goosebumps" kind of testimony. I'm just making the point that probably many of us enter ministry with mixed motives, which may even enhance our ministries. What do I mean by that?

First, it helps us ministers to understand that most people function out of mixed motives. Sometimes I have heard and preached sermons on commitment that have drawn a sharp line in the sand and said, "You have two choices. You may be totally committed, or if not, you are totally uncommitted." I am not criticizing the strong call of Jesus to give ourselves to him as the center of our lives, but few of us function with that kind of purity of heart. If my choices are to be totally committed, completely called or not called at all, then I have little choice. I know myself well enough to understand I am a mixed bag, and I need to be aware of that. I am a minister because forty years from that first nudging, I still feel impressed to do this. But frankly, there are days when I wonder if I took the right road. Could I have been an attorney like my brother? What if I had spent the same amount of educational work in preparing for a business career? What if I had chosen another vocational road?

I know there are some folks who seem to function with absolute certainty about God's will. There is no mystery at all to their journeys. The call is crystal clear. For many of us, however, life possesses more ambiguity and anguish. We do not possess all the answers, and we have to live with our questions. A lot of us live that way, which is alright. With the best light we have, we make our choices and choose the road we will travel. We trust God to travel with us. We do not live with the constant fear that at some point we took the wrong direction, and at that point God abandoned us. What an awful view of God. It really suggests that I am responsible for making all the right choices, and if I choose wrong, God leaves me to myself. Many of us who are ministers experience some profound ambivalence about our calling. Some days we wonder if we are making any difference. Some days we offer our gifts to people, and we feel rejected. We can even understand the anguish of Jesus who felt separated from the Heavenly Parent, and Jesus' words become ours, "My God, my God, why have you forsaken me?" Yet, we move on knowing that a great part of the call is the promise of Jesus never to leave us or forsake us.

Our uncertainty as ministers may help us to connect more intimately with our hearers who also experience their uncertainty. But there is an even more crucial thing that our self-awareness does for us. We may recognize more clearly how much we depend upon God. All of us need some assurance and some certainty for our lives. We simply cannot live with any peace or purpose if everything is up for grabs. Without faith that God is with us on the journey, we become immobilized.

However, absolute assurance that we know clearly everything God intends for us can lead to a tragic arrogance. We forget our need for God. We believe that our ways are God's ways, and God's ways are our ways. The distance between the divine and the human collapses, and we begin to assume we are like God. Much religious fundamentalism gives this impression. The problem is not that people believe things passionately. The problem is, they believe them presumptuously. To believe that we know everything about God's direction is to reduce God to our size and ultimately to create God in our image.

While fundamentalism assumes it knows too much, some forms of religious liberalism offer very little to people for their lives. The distance between the creator and creation is too vast. Humankind can't live on the bread of ambiguity alone. Most people want a faith that respects reason, but let's remember we are dealing with the leap of faith. We ministers deal with words such as grace, love, sin, and forgiveness. We are calling ourselves and others not just to define the terms but to live out of these realities. Who among us, for example, can ever explain grace in such a way that it becomes a reasonable concept? The fact is, it is not reasonable. Grace is throwing a party for a

75

prodigal son who hardly deserves it. The radicality of Jesus' message is sabotaged unless we can receive by faith some truths for our lives.

The calling of God fits the same category. We take one step, and we trust God to walk beside us as we take the next. We make no pretense to pure and perfect motives. A part of faith is trusting that God takes our need for love, our desire to be liked, our impulse to please, along with our wanting to do God's work and will and moves with us into the places where we will serve. We trust God, not ourselves.

One of the wonderful experiences in life is to meet someone who comes to know us and who loves us. I never cease to be amazed at the unconditional love I receive from my wife. Diane knows me better than any other person. She has seen me be kind, caring, and generous. Diane has also seen me when I have acted selfishly, have said unkind things, and have done things I later regretted. Yet, Diane's steady love has never wavered.

Before I was married, I wondered if anybody could love me if that person really knew me. Since I have been a minister, most people have seen me as a public person. I have worked hard to try to perfect that part of me. Making a good impression has been high on my list of priorities. But what if people really knew me? I wasn't a bad person, but I could disappoint myself with some of the things I said or did. What if someone really knew me beneath the spit polished exterior? Would that person reject me? Would I be abandoned? I never cease to be amazed at the unconditional love that embraces me from the human being who knows me best.

In a profound sense, much of my spiritual journey has been to open myself to the unconditional love of the One the mystics called the Divine Lover. While I have been able to articulate the words of God's grace, I have struggled to receive that goodness and to live out of that trust. In many ways the love of Diane has been the prism though which I have come to a new view of the graciousness of God.

You may be asking, "Well, that's all nice, but what does that story have to do with preaching?" My answer is everything. If we come to the pulpit only with our resources, we run great dangers. If we happen to be good at speaking, we risk that kind of ego-driven preaching that is constantly thinking of new ways to make us more appealing. We are apt to become cute and clever, trying to outdo ourselves each time we come to the pulpit. While there is nothing wrong with appropriate creativity, the means must always serve the end of preaching. That is, we have a life-changing message to share. Our job is not to call attention to the vessel but rather to the precious cargo we are trying to bring to the shores of people's lives.

Preaching does have a performative quality to it, but the danger is when it becomes our performance. Most of us who preach know the anxiety and exhaustion that come when preaching loses the vertical dimension of our call by God and becomes only a horizontal transaction between the listeners and us. We become driven to top what we did the week before, and our mood rises and falls on the responses we receive at the door. This is a particularly dangerous temptation in our times. Most people like to be entertained. As I have said, boring is not synonymous with faithful proclamation. Yet, if putting on a good show becomes the compelling force behind our worship and our witness in words, we open ourselves to seeing the most crucial component of the Christian's experience as being fundamentally a human enterprise. The name of God may be yanked into the worship service. We may invoke pious jargon, but the pressure to perform is the real guiding force.

The sense of call from God is a reminder to those of us who preach both of the ground of our being and the ground of our doing. Rather than seeing the call as a once-in-time event, we understand it as an ongoing promise of God's presence. We journey by faith. We venture ahead with all of the mixture of motives that are a part of us. Yet, the presence of the Holy One does not depend on our having to get it all right. In the best way we can, we offer ourselves to serve. The call does not depend on the servant, however, but on the master. We trust the unconditional love of the One who has promised never to leave or forsake us. Thus, we live and preach out of the intimacy of the God who loves us for who we are. We can speak more authentically about being related to God because we aren't afraid that our relationship is fragile, constructed on the always accurate calculation of what God wants.

Compassion

Calling is our awareness of the God who is with us through the thick and thin—the God whose presence is not predicated on our perceiving perfectly some kind of plan we presume God has for us. We move with the best light we have. We offer ourselves to God through prayer. Yet, we are fallible. Because the promise of God's presence is secure, we, therefore, do not live wondering if somewhere in the past we made a wrong turn, and God left us in the process. We preach to people with awareness that they, too, often second-guess their decisions. They wonder if and where God is. We can preach to them with the assurance that on this pilgrim journey, wherever we are, that other name for the Gracious One is Emmanuel, God with us.

This leads me to a second quality that is essential: compassion. Ministers usually think of compassion as a quality we exercise toward others. Some become very good at this type of compassion. Relating to others, these ministers are forgiving, offering, and loving. They are kind, gentle, and patient. Folks who are wounded flock to their offices because they feel close to and cared for by these caregivers.

But what about compassion for ourselves as ministers? What about forgiveness, love, and patience? The fact is, some of us are much better at giving than receiving. No wonder we become angry, depressed, and feel enormously distant from God and from others. The more we batter ourselves as not adequate, the less intimate we feel with God. We save others, but we do not save ourselves. As Thoreau reminded us, we become persons of "quiet desperation," maybe going through the motions of ministry but missing any sense of meaning.

Many of us who go into ministry are reminded by others what a "high and holy calling" we have. Implied in that phrase is the expectation that we will model all the great virtues in our lives. Recently, I was traveling through the Charlotte, North Carolina, airport to make a connection to another city. For one of the few times I can recall, I had some extra time and didn't have to sprint from one gate to the other. I stopped to buy a magazine, and a very nice woman helped me. "Are you from Charlotte?" she asked. "No, I live in Richmond, but I used to be a minister in Charlotte," I said. Understand that I do not usually volunteer such information about my vocation because I often have to listen to stories about people who used to go to church and why they quit.

For whatever reason, though, I told this kind woman in Charlotte what I did. The expression on her face can only be described as a "heavenly glow." "That's so wonderful," she said, and proceeded to tell the other woman behind the counter. Now I was staring at two heavenly glows and a double, "That's wonderful!" I decided this was not the time to complain about the inflated prices airport vendors charge.

I do not want to overstate the case. Except when Jimmy Swaggart or Jim and Tammy Bakker are grabbing the headlines, I am glad to be known as a minister. The women in the airport were kind and affirming. They could have told me that their husbands didn't go to church, and what did I suggest to make them attend. I have been met by those kinds of questions, and I have been tempted to say, "Sorry, I'm off duty." These women did make me feel good. If I had told them I worked for the IRS, I doubt they would have been so glad.

In a small way, this episode in Charlotte captures the view some people have of ministers. Mind you, there are those people who believe we could not make it in any other profession so we chose something benign like ministry. Yet, when we identify ourselves as ministers, we are immediately identified as people who exemplify the finest qualities of life. When I talk about compassion, however, I really want to speak about the expectations we have of ourselves.

Let's begin by recognizing that we should have some expectations. If I meet somebody for the first time, and the first words out of my mouth are, "I'm a minister, but remember I'm only human," it reveals a lot about me. I hope the person standing in front of me recognizes I am human. While the women in the airport shop were impressed with my vocation, I doubt they had any illusion I was perfect. There's something bizarre about a minister who seems to have to remind everybody she is just like them. Some ministers use the language of the locker room as frequently as the language of Zion. Why is it necessary for me to prove that the only four-letter words I know are not love and hope? I get uncomfortable around ministers who seem bent on destroying the perceived stereotype of preachers and who do everything they can to prove they are not like all the other clergy.

We are the clergy. While most people recognize our humanity and accept our foibles and failures graciously, they do expect some consistency between our talk and our walk. For most of us, our own humanity is very evident even without our intentionally working at it. People are usually turned off by a kind of stiff, superpious preacher, but that doesn't mean we have to make deliberate displays of our humanness just so people will think we are real.

My deeper concern, however, is with those of us who have learned to articulate the gospel of compassion but who have a difficult time internalizing it. The ironic heart of the message we bear as preachers is that we are called to live in a way none of us can fully live. We are always speaking between the ideal of what we are called to be and the reality of what we are. For example, we preach about the "peace that passeth understanding." Every Sunday some people come to the church house seeking a sanctuary. Their lives are cluttered; their schedules are frantic; some of them are overextended financially. They have trouble sleeping at night and live their days with the knot of anxiety in the pit of their stomachs. Some of them aren't sure what they really need except relief from the worry. We, as ministers, stand in the pulpit and fashion words about a peace that can still us in our storms. They are good words. They are biblical words. Yet, for some of us who preach, we know the gap that exists between what we preach and what we practice.

Several months ago I came home from the office. The children in our neighborhood were playing in front of our house. One of the little girls was obviously in charge. "I'm the mommy," she said. "You're the daddy; you're the sister," and so on she went until every child was a part of the pretend family. Watching these children took me back in time. I used to pretend to be Superman. My mother would give me an old towel that became my cape. A white t-shirt with a crayoned "S" on the front was my uniform. Since there was no kryptonite near my house, I was more than sufficient for anything. I didn't leap from any tall buildings in a single bound, but I did jump from some rocks with my towel blowing in the breeze. Of course, my mother had a way of jolting me back to reality. "Come to supper," she called. "Yes ma'am," I replied, and off came the t-shirt and towel. Once again I was "Chuck" as my parents reminded me to eat my green beans and to keep my elbows off the table.

The days of pretending to be superhuman are over. As a child, my mother would call me back to reality. As an adult, I call myself back to the reality that I am a minister, but more fundamentally that I am a human being. I come to the pulpit not because I have arrived at the finish line well ahead of everyone else. I am speaking to people who are running this marathon of life with me, and we stumble, struggle, gasp for air, and nurse our pains as we move toward "the prize of the high calling." The issue is this: How do we as proclaimers be gentle and kind to ourselves so that we do not quit the race because of frustration and fatigue? How do we treat ourselves with the same compassion that we preach the gracious God has toward others?

Obviously, this question has been dealt with extensively. I want to make one suggestion that relates to preaching: We understand ourselves not only as speakers of our sermons, but also as listeners. In fact, I do not believe we can preach authentically to people until and unless we recognize our need for the message. Somehow the impression is given in the training of ministers that we are being equipped to provide people with answers. The therapeutic model is frequently invoked. People come to us with their problems, and we guide them to try to arrive at the right decision. Sometimes the medical model is employed. We are told that preachers are like physicians. Physicians listen to patients' symptoms, make diagnoses, and write illegible prescriptions. Ministers listen to their parishioners' symptoms, but instead of physical pain, they deal with diseases of the spirit. Preaching is when they offer the prescription. Of course, preachers, unlike physicians, are expected to be clear in offering the prescription

These models fail to recognize that we preachers are both physicians *and* patients. When we do not see this, we forget the humanity we share with our listeners and our need to hear again and again the good news. When I preach about the peace of God, for example, I listen closely to the text because I share much of the anxiety of those in the congregation. My own life is too cluttered; my schedule is too full; I often overextend myself. If I approach preaching as if I have appropriated all of the truth I preach, I am being both dishonest and foolish. I will either learn to live with the delusion, or I will forsake the ministry because I have overexpected and become weary of the charade. Therefore, in the training of preachers we need to be careful that we do not portray the pulpit as the place where we dispense answers to others' questions or provide prescriptions for others' pain. As Henri Nowen so beautifully said, we who are ministers are the "wounded healers."

I recognize that this view of preaching can be abused. Proclamation is not just writing a prescription for the preacher every Sunday. Hopefully, we don't read the biblical text for Sunday and ask only, "What does this do for me?" Because I may feel overextended in my commitments does not mean everybody who is listening is an extension of me. As we prepare our sermons, we do not turn our offices into a house of mirrors where everything that eventually gets said in the sermon is a reflection of our lives. While all of us do share much in common, we also are different. The hurried pastor who is trying to get himself to slow down is likely to miss the needs of the widow whose grief has caused her to pull the curtains at her house and to withdraw. She spends most of her day staring at the stuffed chair where her husband used to sit. What word does the frantic pastor have for this woman?

As preachers we recognize the diversity of our congregations. Being a listener to our own sermons does not mean that we make every message a means to meet our ends. Yet, we as ministers are both speakers *and* listeners. I want to retain that emphasis because I have seen good preachers give up when they felt it was hypocritical to preach something they had not appropriated for themselves. The fact is, if we are preaching, we are often speaking about things that are still beyond us. If we call the church to justice for women, those of us who are males realize how easy it is to affirm such positions as the full participation of women in ministry but how hard it is to become real agents of change. We call the church to economic justice. "Is it right," we ask, to live in a world where we have more than enough while many have nothing?" Yet, our own closets are filled with clothes, and our own plates are filled with food.

When we preach about pastoral concerns, we also understand that we as preachers are still on the journey. I have often preached from Paul's words to the churches in Rome, "And we know that in all things God works for good to those who love God and live according to God's purpose." Why do I preach this? Do I preach it because I have successfully scaled the summit of this promise? Do I preach it because I live each and every moment of my life this way? I wish that were so. I wish I were able to put the full weight of my being on these powerful words of assurance. The fact is, I often live far from the mountaintop of this promise.

What do I do as a preacher? I have some options. The words are in the Bible. Of course, I can ignore them and move on to the sections of the Bible that seem easier for me to apply. Or I can preach this promise of Paul as if I have internalized it and as if I have arrived at the summit of certainty. By the way, that is a temptation for us ministers. Some people do like absolute certainty. There are those who want to believe that their preachers live beyond the conflict and confusion. They like to think we have no ambiguity and ambivalence but walk out of the seminary with a certificate of certainty. Preachers who believe this usually turn the pulpit into a place to exhort and even to condemn. This kind of proclamation lacks the ring of realness, but most of all, it is dishonest to the parishioners and the preacher.

I preach from Romans 8:28 because I need to say it again to others and to myself. While I want to live this way, I often do not. I wonder why some things happen. I suffer at the setbacks. I shrink from pain. I have a hard time "knowing" that God is working in all things. So when I preach, I speak as a fellow pilgrim. What would it   be like to live in the promise land of this vision? I want to draw all of our focus to the promise to which we aspire and to the power of God that moves us forward. At the same time I want to show compassion for others and for myself. I do not want to reduce the promise to fit the contours of what I already am. We need to be challenged to live more and be more. Yet, I want to remember we are all human beings; we are all pilgrim people, and that means life is a continuing journey toward the city of God.

Hope

Writing books is a lot like fashioning sermons. You always have to say no to some important items in order to say yes to include what you consider to be more important in the sermon. As I thought about what I wanted to say yes to in this section of the book, I thought about hope as a quality of the preacher. Some preachers whom I meet are filled with despair even to the point of being almost immobilized. Ministry is demanding. The multiplicity of tasks most ministers have, the expectations we have of ourselves and others have of us, the lack of a distinct definition of what constitutes success in ministry—these and other factors contribute to a fairly high level of depression among those of us who are clergy. At times our frustration may manifest itself in anger. We become angry with ourselves for not achieving all we had once dreamed. We become angry with our churches because of the pile of details to which we have to attend and the endless rounds of meetings that keep us from doing those things where we find our greatest meaning. We become angry with our families because they are a constant reminder of people who need our care, and we come home too tired to care for those we love the most.

I do not mean to overdraw the problem. Obviously, there is much that is satisfying about being a minister. Most people in churches are not overly demanding, and they are concerned about us as persons. Unfortunately, unhappiness, especially among parish ministers, seems to be on the rise, and those of us who are a part of the church need to examine both what we expect of our ministers and what we can do to encourage them.

This sense of despair reflected in depression or anger obviously affects the preaching of a minister. Preparation of a sermon requires focus and concentration. These prerequisites are hard to come by when we are drowning in the sea of our own sadness or resentment. Additionally, both depression and unresolved anger cause us to feel distant from those around us. We draw the circle tightly around ourselves, and what little energy we have is exhausted in maintaining our own emotional equilibrium. We feel little connection with our listeners and may even view them as the enemies. The speaking of the words in the sermon may become listless; or if we are consumed with rage, the words may be harsh and biting. Even if we do not intend to show our feelings, we are apt to let them slide out in the tone of our voice or in a manner that communicates either, "I don't care about you," or "I don't even like you." It is difficult to communicate intimacy when we feel a great gulf between ourselves and our hearers.

What, then, do we do? We may deny that we experience certain feelings that trouble us. For example, anger is sometimes considered an inappropriate feeling for ministers. Of course, Jesus became angry, but we sometimes lose sight of that as we remind ourselves of the biblical injunction, "Be angry and sin not." I have met people in church who profess never to get angry about anything. "I have never had a cross word with my wife in 45 years of marriage." That is remarkable. I don't think I went 45 hours in my marriage until I said something out of anger. Maybe some people have developed the ability to put the lid on whatever feelings with which they feel uncomfortable. As for me in my house and out of my house, I get angry. I get sad. I get uptight. I get upset. I feel sorry for myself. You get the picture. Feelings arise within us as our response to the ups and downs, the successes and setbacks of our lives. The issue is, "What do we do with these feelings? How do we handle our anger or our sadness?"

Denying that we have these feelings hardly seems to be the best option. Another possibility is to give vent to all of our feelings. We can make the prophet Amos our model for ministry. There's no doubt Amos certainly had the courage of his convictions. Nobody would have asked Amos where he stood on an issue. Amos had no uncertainty about what was right and what was wrong. The prophet began,

"The Lord roars from Zion and thunders from Jerusalem," and as spokesperson for the Lord, Amos also roared and thundered.

Now we may want to applaud Amos for his backbone and admit that he didn't let his indignity fester, but as ministers, we want to be cautious about holding him up as the only model for handling anger. First, it's better to be independently wealthy if you and I are going to imitate the shepherd of Tekoa. Amos' types usually do not last too long in one place. There is only so much "roaring" and "thundering" congregations can take.

Second, we need to ask, "How are people receiving our anger as ministers?" Most folks in the church realize their ministers get angry. Even Jesus got angry as witnessed by those changers in the Temple who probably spent half the night looking for their coins and straightening the furniture. While ministers do get angry, we also model for people how to handle that feeling. Do we become moody and temperamental? Do we withdraw? Do we become passive-aggressive, expressing our anger in indirect and devious ways? Do we turn over the table in the fellowship hall, sending the poor couple who has perfected the painfully slow technique of giving us change at the Wednesday night supper into panic or shock? I know Jesus turned over the tables in the Temple, and I'm certainly not going to criticize Jesus for the way he handled his anger, but I have a hard time holding the scene in the Temple in front of students and saying this is the picture of what to do when you don't like something.

The real question is this: How do we handle our anger or despair? For preachers this is an essential question since those feelings will affect the ways in which we speak the words to people. What I want to suggest is by no means a complete answer to the concern. Other books will deal with ministers' feelings from a pastoral care perspective and will give us more insight into the things that make us deeply sad or deeply angry.

The factor that I want to be a part of our thinking is hope. The minister needs to be a hopeful or "hope-filled" person. Easier said than done. Sure. It costs me nothing to write the word hopeful. What about the young minister who goes to his first church and encounters nothing but resistance. The committee that was responsible for bringing him to the church insisted the congregation wanted change. "For too long," the committee chair had said, "our church has been in decline. Our ministries, such as they are, are stagnant. We want a bright, young pastor who will restore the vision and vitality."

Maybe this young pastor should know better than to take any of us at our word. After all, I have said I wanted to change something about me but was not willing to pay the price. But the church did say it wanted to change. So the young minister pours himself into the parish, but now he can't even find the members of the committee that talked to him. After a year, this promising pastor sits down to take stock. Little has happened to the church, but a lot has happened to him. The dream is dull. His energy is sapped. His preaching lacks the passion that once propelled him to the pulpit. Why preach passionately when it seems nobody wants to share the dream and do the work to make the church in name a church in reality?

I know that hope is easier to write about than to actualize. I was a parish minister long enough to know those days when I lived with quiet despair or seething anger. I experienced those painful moments when the grand dream became dull, and the work of the ministry was just that—work. I do not want to give the impression that I'm walking into the critical care unit where some minister is on the respirator and saying, "All you need is a little hope." I think I know how desperate it can be when, like the prophet Jeremiah, we have spoken all the words we know, and nothings seems to happen.

Yet, I do want to say a word for hope. After all, those of us who are ministers are taught to think theologically. When we face the dark night of our soul, where do we turn to find some light? I suggest hope. In some quarters, hope is a lightweight word. We hope for this and that. I hope the Miami Dolphins win the Super Bowl. You hope Dallas wins. He hopes he will get a date for Saturday night and cares nothing about football. We hope for a new dress, a new car, or a promotion in our job. These things may be important to us, but the word "hope" floats like a butterfly through our vocabularies.

Biblical hope is different. This hope is built on the presence and promise of God. When we gather for a funeral, we listen to the minister speak a word of hope of life beyond death. To those of us gathered in the funeral home, death looks final. The person who once was vibrant is now lifeless. We have a body, but our mother or our sister or our daughter doesn't speak to us. They don't embrace us or kiss us or open their mouths to say again, "I love you." The funeral home director is kind, but he speaks about the person as deceased. As people file into the funeral home for the service, they are handed a card with the name, date of birth, date of death, surviving family members, a few other facts, and at the bottom is a copy of Psalm 23. The psalm does say, "We shall dwell in the house of the Lord forever," but most of us fumble the card in our hands as the organist plays off-key every stanza of "The Old Rugged Cross."

The minister stands and somewhere in her message mentions hope. We check the number of people who are there. "After all, she was old," we say, "and most of her friends have already died. That's why so few are here." The minister turns in her Bible to the fifteenth chapter of First Corinthians. "Where, O death, is your victory? Where, O death, is your sting?" she continues. "The sting of death is sin, and the power of sin is the law. But thanks be to God, who gives us the victory through our Lord Jesus Christ." "Maybe it's the weather." We think that explains the small cluster of folks who are there. The few friends he did have are frail themselves, and this is not a good day for a funeral if there is such a thing as a good day for a funeral."

"But," the minister is saying, "thanks be to God, who gives us the victory through our Lord Jesus Christ." Many of us have been the ministers at those funerals, and we have read the words. I have read the words. In fact, I have read the words so often, I know them by heart. Maybe I know them too well. Actually, these words are absolutely revolutionary and speak about a victorious hope God gives us through our Lord Jesus Christ.

Frankly, I can reduce the impact of these words as well as the next preacher. I can talk about hope with the same fervor I have for mowing the grass. Sometimes I wonder why that happens. Maybe we do deal with holy things so much. Maybe our training as ministers has not emphasized enough the awe and wonder that abiding qualities such as hope should evoke. Or maybe I have done so many funeral services that I can voice the words without appreciating the truth they express. Maybe it is all these things and many more. What I do know, however, is that as ministers we want and need to recover the realities our words represent.

We talk today about giving our listeners back a vocabulary by which they can live. For example, we speak about opening the word "love" to people so that they understand the unconditional way they are loved by God. Take the teenage boy who sits in the balcony of the church. He started doing drugs as a way to get a lift. God knows he needed a lift. When he went home, he faced parents who screamed and yelled. He looked in the mirror and saw a face that was changing. His body was changing, and he didn't understand all the urges he felt. Confused and depressed, a friend told him one day, "Take this, and it will make you feel better." Who doesn't want to feel better?

What will his minister say to him on Sunday? I know it doesn't look as if the young man is paying attention, but he may be hearing more than we think. Remember when you and I were teenagers. Pretending not to listen is a part of the adolescent code. What happened, though, is that once in awhile something filtered through, and we did listen. What do we as ministers say to this young man? Don't do drugs! That is something we need to say. But if we offer nothing substantive to this young man and all the young and older women and men, we likely will not make much difference. How do we speak about love so that God's unconditional care is heard? How do we bring our hearers inside of those stories where people who did not love themselves were dramatically changed by the awareness that to be loved by the Christ and in Christ and through Christ was to find a new ground for being? How do we, as preachers, give searching people a vocabulary whose words written into the scripts of our lives give us a new center?

The word "hope" is like that. How do we not only say it, but also receive its reality for ourselves? In the Bible hope is about the presence and promise of God. It is about a future whose shape we do not know but is lived into with the belief that God is working in the process. Yet, hope is more than just a faith in the future. Hope is believing that God is working with us in the moment because the past, present, and future all melt into the time in which God works. In a way, hope is about moving on even when we do not feel like it because hope is more about what God can do than what we are asked to do.

I no longer live in Charlotte. I assume the man who marked my suits is still there. "I don't mean to make you feel bad," he would say, "but we are all different." One size doesn't fit all.

What's true for clothes is true for the clergy. We are different. Some things, however, are needed by all of us. Hope—that's one. We go out to change the world, but we have trouble changing ourselves. Do we give up or go on? If we look to ourselves, I believe the answer will be "give up." That is why hope is the eye of the heart looking to the "author and finisher of our faith." I sometimes forget. I need to remember. God is in this with us. We move from now to later, from the present to whatever the future may be. I call that hope.

Questions for Reflection

1. How would you describe your "call" to preach? What do you do to keep fresh that sense of call?

2. How compassionate are you toward yourself? Why do those of us in ministry have a more difficult time forgiving ourselves than we do in forgiving others?

3. Write down some of the things that may cause you as a minister to experience despair. How much of that despair is caused or accentuated by the demands you put on yourself? What would you look like and sound like if you were a preacher with a genuine sense of hope rooted in the presence of God?

Sermon

Don't Rob Yourself of the Joy

Luke 4:14-21
Tiffany Greer Hamilton

In Luke's account of the ministry of Jesus, we have Jesus who has just come from his baptism and temptation in the wilderness. We find him beginning his ministry in Galilee. Early one Saturday morning Jesus returned to Nazareth to speak in the synagogue. His friends, relatives, and neighbors gathered in great excitement. They had watched him grow to manhood. They knew his parents, Mary and Joseph. So they were astonished at his air of authority as he strode to the center of the crowded stone room and was handed the book of the prophet Isaiah from the Torah shrine. He found the passage he wanted and then read the ancient prophecy:

> The Spirit of the Lord is upon me, because he has anointed me to bring good news to the poor. He has sent me to proclaim release to the captives and recovery of sight for the blind, to let the oppressed go free, to proclaim the year of the Lord's favor.

Jesus handed the scriptures back to the attendant and stared quietly at the rows of townspeople. "Today," he said slowly, "this scripture has been fulfilled in your hearing."

As Jesus was teaching in the synagogue, he had a purpose in what he read. He did not flip open the scriptures to see on which passage it would land. No, he chose this passage from Isaiah 61 because he was announcing who he really was. He was speaking to his "home church." They thought they knew him, but he announced to them that their Jesus of Nazareth is Jesus the Christ; this son of Joseph is the son of God; this carpenter is the long-awaited Messiah. Jesus reads to them that he has been anointed by the Spirit. He has been called to be the prophet of whom Isaiah spoke.

In his reading, Jesus not only reveals who he is, but also what his ministry will be about. It will be a ministry of action: preaching, healing, releasing, proclaiming. It will begin in Nazareth with his own people. This ministry will be one of social concern, moral transformation, and spiritual restoration. But when will it begin? Verse 21 reveals that it will begin today. We read, "*Today* this scripture has been fulfilled in your hearing."

The crowd was filled with awe at the words they heard. They were excited. Was Jesus claiming that their hopes were to be realized? Today? Can you imagine being part of that crowd, hearing Jesus proclaim his calling—a calling you are a part. Do you remember hearing God announcing your call to mission? Think back to when you realized that you were called to be a Christian, to be a part of Jesus' ministry. I was so excited about this new adventure. I was anxious as I started sorting out what it all meant. I was also afraid. How could I be called? But I was sure I had heard the call, "Today, this scripture has been fulfilled in *your* hearing."

Every day is a today. We need to hear this voice each day to maintain our call. We need to spend time listening to the voice of God. Have you ever thought about the devotional time we call "quiet time"? We are to take time and be quiet before God, listen to God's voice, and learn the call of the Spirit. Jesus was anointed by the Spirit to carry on the mission of God. We are also anointed by the Spirit. This Spirit was with Jesus and is with us. In John 15:26 Jesus calls the Holy Spirit a counselor, a helper sent by the Father to teach us all things and bring to our remembrance all things that Jesus has said. The Spirit works through us, beyond us, ahead of us, and behind us. That Spirit speaks to us, encourages us, and guides us along this mission journey. We just have to recognize and listen to the call.

Several years ago my grandfather developed Alzheimer's disease. It got to the point where he could not recognize anyone, that is, except one person—my grandmother. She could be two rooms away, but when she heard her voice, he would say, "CC, CC." He knew her voice—the voice of the person who spoke to him, who took care of him, who loved him more than anyone. That is the way it is when we learn the voice of God. No matter what the obstacle, frustration, or weariness we have before us, we can always return to the familiar voice that loves us, cares for us and calls us to ministry. "Today, this scripture has been fulfilled in your *hearing*."

Now what? Well, if we follow the proclamation of Jesus, we are called to action. Hearing brings action. When you hear the alarm clock sound, you get up and turn if off. When you hear the phone ring, you answer it. When you hear someone sneeze, you respond with "Bless you." When you listen to your radio and your favorite song comes on, you can't help but sing.

When I was a child, my three brothers and I would get on our bikes and ride around for what seemed like hours and miles away from home. Sometimes we would stay out a little late—at least until dinner time. My mother could not call us home by yelling; we were too far away. So she devised a method for getting us home for dinner. She would stand on the back porch and ring this huge, black cattle bell. It did not matter where we were or how far away we were, we could hear that bell ringing. Mom was calling us home for dinner. And you better believe when we heard that bell, we would peddle home as fast as we could. Hearing leads to action. "Today, this scripture has been *fulfilled* in your hearing."

All this talk about hearing and action makes me wonder if we realize what we are getting ourselves into when we accept Jesus and his ministry? The Gospels are full of Jesus' ministry: feeding the five thousand, healing the sick, loving the unlovable, forgiving unconditionally. Is Jesus saying we are supposed to do those things? Jesus said he was called to preach, proclaim, release, bring recovery of sight, and announce the year of the Lord. Are we supposed to do those things, too? This list may seem overwhelming. You may be saying, "I can't do that." Or "Who has time for all of that? Between work, family, and friends, I barely have time to sleep." Or "I don't have the resources to help others; I don't even know what to do."

When you really get down to it, this mission just sounds too hard. Its sounds like a lot of work. Or does this mission sound like a gift? God loved us so much that He gave Jesus to die for us. God loved us so much that He included us in the mission. We are given the opportunity to be part of something bigger than we are. We can be a part of a divine plan. God needs us to be His feet, His hands, and His face. We are given the gift of experiencing the joy of giving.

When I go home to visit my parents, they usually take me out to eat. They offer to pay and after several minutes of arguing over the bill, my parents usually end up paying. Sometimes my mom will say, "You need a new dress," and she'll take me to buy that dress even if I say, "I don't need it," or "You don't have to do that." The catch phrase my parents say during these discussions is "Don't rob me of the joy." It's kind of a joke now because every time we talk about a gift they say, "Don't rob me of the joy."

Jesus speaks to us today as he did that Saturday morning in Galilee. He looks at each of us and says, "Today, this scripture has been fulfilled in your hearing." Jesus is saying, "Accept this gift, and don't rob yourself of the joy."

Chapter 4

Connecting with the Bible

What do we preach? Those of us who are ministers know this question can be approached in at least two ways. First, there is the practical consideration of what does a minister in a church preach each Sunday. Those of us who have "been there and done that" know how difficult it is to have something fresh and forceful every week. The demands of most churches are heavy. The minister may find himself in the middle of a multitude of demands that take not only a strong investment of time but also a heavy emotional drain. Attending a committee meeting exacts a certain toll. Preaching a funeral has its emotional requirement. Even something as joyful as a wedding takes both time and energy as the minister finds herself in the midst of families who want everything to be "just right."

These examples only scratch the surface of the breadth and depth of things a parish minister does. Preaching, therefore, is done in the mix and mingle of many other activities. We are called to explore biblical texts and to fashion words for the Sunday sermon while we are administrating, comforting, meeting, and doing countless other things. No wonder some ministers feel frustrated when it comes to shaping the sermon for Sunday. That may be one reason why effective preachers develop a process for preparation that maximizes the time available and why these same ministers learn to utilize small chunks of time for reading and thinking.

What do we peach? This question raises the specter of the sermon that will be preached on Sunday and the need to be prepared. But there is a second issue this question raises. What is the source of our sermons? Where do we find the essential elements of what we want to say? Simply, I want to respond—in the Bible. In the anthology of literature we call the biblical canon we find the persons, the stories, and especially the God who give shape to our lives.

Interestingly, this renewal of biblical preaching comes at a time when several denominations are mired in "battles for the Bible." We are witnessing a resurgence of religious fundamentalism in our time that claims not only to believe the Bible absolutely but also to interpret it infallibly. It is too bad that this kind of reactionary view of the

Bible has sometimes been identified with the term "biblical preaching." Some of us believe very strongly in the spiritual authority of the Bible, but we certainly do not view it as a book of science or geography or allow its ancient contours to dictate our cosmology. Certain fundamentalists have made a living by making statements such as, "If you don't believe everything in the Bible, you can't believe anything." While that judgment sounds pious, the whole argument depends on what we mean by the word "believe." Do we need to believe that everything is literally true? No one really believes that. Jesus said, "I am the door." Of course, he was speaking symbolically, and once you have said that, you then leave the way open to interpret other things symbolically.

Interpreting the Bible in a flat, literalistic way is an invitation to minimize the power and authority of Scripture. It leaves us debating whether Adam and Eve were real people rather than seeing the full force of the Genesis story—that God is the creator of all of life. We argue about whether the world really began in 4004 BC and then try to figure out how the dinosaurs fit. In the process we lose the grandeur of a God who is behind a cosmos that is wonderfully inextricable. Fundamentalism is reductionistic. It wants to know and to explain what is ultimately beyond our full knowing and certainly beyond our complete explaining. What we lose is the sense of awe and wonder as we seek to create God in an image we can understand. Consequently, our preaching loses the wonder that comes when we enter the biblical text and become alive to its shaping power. As preachers, our calling is not to be defense attorneys for the Bible. We are not apologists arguing for the veracity of Scripture. Rather, we are called to be led by the Spirit of God as we explore the text and as we give voice to the truth that can set us free. With these things said, I want to speak about the Bible from two directions.

The Bible as Distant

To understand the Bible, we begin by recognizing that it has a certain distance from our lives. Since what we call the "books" of the Bible were fashioned in different times and ways, these books emerge from cultures and cosmologies different from ours. For example, the world of the apostle Paul is different from the one in which we live. If we do not recognize that difference, we will attempt to transfer Paul's worldview into our time and in the process distort the real message of the Bible. Paul seems to believe or at least to accept the custom of slavery. In the letter to the Ephesians, the Apostle instructs slaves on how to obey their masters and masters on how to treat their slaves. While we can give Paul credit for helping slave owners of his day to have a more caring attitude toward those they owned, the fact is that the apostle Paul never challenged the institution of slavery. In this way at least, Paul seemed to be captive to an institution of his time.

The issue is what do we as proclaimers do with something like this. Believing that the Bible in its entirety can simply be laid over our time as a pattern creates serious problems. Do we want to affirm slavery as an institution? Fortunately, Christians have come to see the inherent wrongness of any system in which a person owns or exploits another person. Our Christian faith has helped us to see the tragedy of slavery. Since we are all created in the image of God and we are called to live to the fullness of that image, we reject slavery as contrary to the creative purpose of God. We have come to possess enough distance from something Paul accepted to see that it is inherently unchristian.

What about the cosmology of much of the Bible? Demons seemed to be accepted in Jesus' day as the cause of what we now understand as mental illness. While persons having the condition were often isolated and feared by others, Jesus reached out to them with compassion. Is that not the real message—to care for people with accepting love? The issue is not demons. The understanding of mental illness has grown dramatically in recent years. We now have insight into the chemistry of the brain and into our own behavior that was not available to the writers of the Bible. Are we really affirming the most significant truths of the biblical message when we speak about demons at work in the lives of people or when we promote a notion that illness is related to sin? The fact is, we twist the most important truths when we are unable to gain sufficient distance from the worldview of another day. Instead of seeing the deeper truths couched in the language and thought of their times, we begin to argue for the acceptance of the forms in which those truths appear. The result is that we have to commit intellectual suicide in order to affirm the Bible as the word of God.

Appropriate distance allows us to view the Bible in its cultural context and to identify those things that are reflective of the culture. An example would be Paul's admonition that a bishop or deacon should be the "husband of one wife." This phrase has been used to exclude women from service either as deacons or as clergy. But consider the first century, the time in which the Apostle lived. It was a patriarchal society. Women had few rights or options. Many regarded women more as property than as persons. Given that cultural context, what would we expect Paul to say? Would we expect him to say "the husband of one wife or the wife of one husband?" That may have been helpful to the role of women in ministry if Paul had said that, but it would have been totally out of character with the world in which Paul lived. Hopefully, we have grown beyond the first-century view of women. Increasingly, women are seen as persons created by God who should not be limited in their call simply on the basis of their gender. Are we really doing justice to the whole message of the Bible when we believe that we can make no interpretation of the Bible in the light of new information and new insights?

Contrary to the cries of some, this is not setting our culture above the Bible or depreciating in any way the fact that the Bible is the Word of God and the Word to us from God. Instead, it is the sensible thing to do. Moreover, simply moving the words from one time period to another does not ensure that we have preserved the message. Unless we have enough distance from the Bible to see the text in its context and then to interpret it in our context with the knowledge and wisdom God gives us, we may wind up with a message that is contrary to the thrust of the entire Bible. Those of us who live in the southern United States do well to remember that many well-meaning preachers in our area in the 1800s used certain verses in the Bible to buttress their support of slavery. They simply transported the words, without giving attention to the worldview of the time in which the words were written, into their own context, repeated the words, and called it biblical preaching. Is that what we want? Is that really biblical preaching? We need to have enough distance from the Bible so that we can see the bigger picture and then "rightly divide the word of truth."

A second factor that may help those of us who preach is to remind ourselves that we do not proclaim the Bible. Rather, we proclaim the truths that are revealed in the Bible and especially the God who reveals God's self. While we come to understand through the Bible about God's care for creation and redemptive love for all God's children, there is also much we do not comprehend. We cannot fully know who God is or explain all of the ways in which God acts. The Hebrew Bible reminds us that "God's ways are not our ways," and Paul confessed his limits when he told the Corinthians, "Now we see through a glass dimly." For those of us who preach, this means we always preach beyond ourselves. Instead of trying to "possess" the God of the Bible, we point to this God who is always beyond us and resist the temptation to restrict God to the categories we can comprehend.

When I was a pastor, I enjoyed the week called "Vacation Bible School." The children came, and they brought laughter to the halls of the church. They also brought something else—their fresh insight into God. One day I was walking by the room where some small children were singing. I stopped outside the door to listen. I had heard the song before, but I always need to hear it again. "God is so high," the children's voices sang, "you can't get over Him. God is so low, you can't get under Him. God is so wide you can't get around Him." When the children had finished, I thanked them. They reminded me of something I needed to hear.

Why is it that I want to whittle God down to a manageable image? Why is it that I am tempted to lose my own wonder at a God who is so high, and low, and wide and then preach as if I have cornered God and can describe all of the ways of this wondrous God. For preachers, nothing is more dangerous to us spiritually than for us to worship a God whom we have fashioned and formed—a God who moves only in ways we order and who is bound to the limited boundaries of our imaginations. Nothing is more dangerous to preaching than to proclaim such a diminished God.

In our day we seem to be witnessing a recovery of the "mystical" element of our faith. This is true not only for Christians but also for many of the world's religions. Many people seem to want more than simply a set of propositions to which they can give mental assent. They want more than a God whom they can know about; they want a God whom they can know and to whom they can relate. They seem to be searching for a relationship to the God of their faith. While those of us who preach are calling people to this more intimate relationship with God, we need to be careful that in trying to make the divine more accessible, we do not preach a deity who is so much with us that this God loses both difference and distance from us. The biblical writers spoke of both the presence and absence of God. This was their way of stressing that at the same time God is invested in human life, God is also the Holy Other. This is the power of preaching. When we come to the pulpit, we do not come with a God whom we possess or can explain. We do not preach a God who bends to the winds of our ways. We proclaim a God who is beyond us, a God who in the words of the children is so high, so low, so wide that neither our minds nor our words can fully embrace or express all that God is.

The Bible as Intimate

What does it mean to see the Bible as intimate? What does it mean to engage the Bible and to be engaged by its messages so that the Bible becomes for us the "lively word of God?" Frankly, I have never had too much problem respecting the appropriate distance of the Bible. As a child, I remember looking at the cover of the small Bible I had and reading the words, "Holy Bible." I certainly did not understand all that "Holy" meant, but I did know that book was different. Our family always had a family Bible on the living room table. While we didn't read from it very much, our family did treat it with reverence. For anyone visiting our home, the Bible was the visual symbol that we were a family of faith. When the living room was cleaned, the Bible was always lovingly dusted like a cherished piece of furniture.

When I received my first Bible and opened its pages, I still felt overwhelmed. (At that time we thought the King James Version came

100

from Jesus' brother, so the KJV was "standard issue" at our house.) When I opened the Bible, I confronted a vocabulary of "Thees and Thous." I had no idea about the variety of literature in the Bible. I read the Psalms in the same way that I read the books of Matthew and Revelation. I had no idea who a lot of the people were in the Bible and certainly had no inkling how some of the names were pronounced. Our pastor told us that the Bible was the Word of God, which I accepted without question or much understanding.

Going to college and seminary, of course, expanded my understanding of the Bible and helped me to appreciate much about its background and the history of the various literature in the Bible. The historical-critical method dominated much of the approach of my professors. While I continue to appreciate this method as one way to approach scripture, I have also come to see its limiting potential. I was taught that the way to approach a biblical text was to view it in its historical context and to discover what it meant in its original setting. That was the exegetical process. Once you discovered what it meant, you then tried to move the ancient meaning into contemporary times and interpret that one meaning for people.

Frankly, this almost sole reliance on the historical-critical method served to increase my distance from the text. As a preacher, I was so eager to find what the text meant, I allowed no room for my imagination and never considered that a text may be polyvalent, or open to several valid interpretations. Every Sunday I preached, I had a horrible fantasy that one of my biblical professors from seminary would slip into the sanctuary to hear my sermon and then tell me at the door that I had missed the message. I was reluctant to engage a text with my imagination because I was intimidated by commentaries that sat on my shelf written by biblical scholars much more knowledgeable than I. In the process my fundamental encounter in the exegetical process was with the commentaries on the biblical text rather than with the biblical text itself, which further accentuated distance.

The Bible as Present

Today more emphasis is being placed on the fact that a biblical text has both a "now" and a "then." The text has a past, but it also has a present. Those of us who preach are called to proclaim the words in relation to people now, thereby opening up the process of biblical interpretation. Rather than seeing a passage of scripture as a "corpse" that once had life, we see it as "living, moving, and being"—intersecting people's lives in the present. The interpreter is not a mortician saying, "Let's discover what once gave this text life and what it meant long ago." Rather, we engage, encounter, and experience the biblical words, and then when we come to preach, we speak of it as the "lively Word of God."

This approach to proclamation is predicated on the idea that the Bible contains the "alive" word of God, which means the Bible is still interpreting itself as the words meet our lives. This gives latitude to the preacher as she engages the biblical text in her study, and then as she shapes her encounter with the Bible into the words that speak to her listeners. While the text in its original setting informs her conclusions, it is only one of the components operative in her inquiry and interpretation. As a proclaimer, she is also asking, "What does this text say?" She operates with the assumption that the Bible contains the "alive" word of God, and thus has a "now" *and* a "then."

Obviously, there are dangers with this approach to interpreting Scripture. When I tell the students in my preaching class to approach a biblical text imaginatively, I try to caution them that this doesn't mean "any interpretation goes." When I say to them that I want them to use the historical-critical method but not to be dependent upon it exclusively, I recall my own training and how my own approach to interpretation was shaped by this "historical excavating" of the text. I was taught to honor what the text meant in its own context, to try to recover that, and then to give shape to those insights in preaching. Now I am telling the students and myself to be more imaginative and to let the biblical word loose from its historical moorings.

I am willing to run this risk because I believe the Bible has a present and also because I believe we need more preaching in which the minister feels more personally connected to the words he speaks. This approach generates intimacy both in the preparation of the sermon and the preaching of the sermon. Recently I had a student preach a sermon from Luke 23:33-43, which is the story of Jesus' dying on the cross, including the reactions of the criminals who were crucified with Jesus. This young woman centered her sermon on the words of one of the thieves to Jesus: "Remember me when you come into your kingdom." She gave us the context of these words and even helped us to understand the notion of "paradise." Jesus had told the penitent thief, "Today you will be with me in paradise."

The thrust of my student's sermon, however, was on the word "remember" and how the criminal's request touched the need of all of us to be remembered. With a sense of amazement, she pointed out that Jesus not only had granted the man's desire to be remembered but also gave him much more "Today, you will be with me . . .," and whatever else paradise may be, it is the experience of being with the Holy One of God both in memory and in presence.

What impressed me about this woman's sermon was the amazement she conveyed at both the question and Jesus' answer. She knew her audience. We were seminary students and a preaching professor. We are the professional "holy people." Our calling is to remind listeners that they are remembered and not forgotten. We tell others that the last word is not an ugly hill with the stench of death. Ours is not a God who stays dead. While we know there are stretches of our journey where God may seem absent, still we proclaim God's presence. We confront struggles by preaching about a God who is with us and who calls us to be with God. We even dare to say to people, "Today, this day, in this moment in time, your life can be changed."

Yet, who often forgets the message that we are remembered? Seminary students and their preaching professor were listening closely to a lively retelling of an old story because in our rush to save others, don't we often lose ourselves? We want to be remembered. We want to be remembered by others. It helps to know that what we are doing makes a difference to people. We didn't go into ministry because we thought we would get a lot of "things." We have become used to buying cars that get more gas mileage to the dollar. We don't live in gated communities. We go to stores that are having sales. This is all right. What we really want to know is whether our words, our lives, our ministries are being remembered. Are we helping people to know there is meaning, or are we a voice crying in the wilderness or someone making noises that make no difference.

My preaching student captured us that day because she understood her need and our need. She perceived how empowering Jesus' words could be for us. We want to be remembered, and we want to live out of a sense of transcendent presence. As ministers, we don't want to preach only the memory of a God who has died for us. We have to face enough without believing that what we say or do makes no ultimate difference.

The first funeral I ever preached was for a child—a baby. I was still in college. The senior minister was out of town. "The family is Baptist," the funeral home director told me on the telephone. "They don't belong to a local church. The family needs a minister." I told him this would be my first funeral. "I'll guide you," he said. "I'll show you where to stand, how to walk in front of the small casket when the funeral procession arrives at the cemetery." It was a hot summer day in Florida. I was perspiring in my standard white shirt and black suit. The director positioned me at the head of the casket. I read the words from the 23rd Psalm, "Yea though I walk through the valley of the shadow of death, I will fear no evil for Thou art with me."

After the funeral I went back to my small apartment and wondered if that was going to be what ministry was like. What do you say to parents, to grandparents, to a family where a child who barely lived has died? Do you open the Bible and read the words of the psalmist as if they are a faint echo from a God who used to be vibrant but who now is either gone or missing in action. When we treat the Bible as the "old" book about a God who once was active but now is on the sidelines, we not only do the Bible a disservice, but we also rob ourselves of any transcendent presence and power to meet the tragedies of our lives. That is what I liked about my young student's sermon. When she opened the Bible and started to speak, she was preaching with a sense that the biblical text had both a present and a past. Sure, these words were first spoken by and to a dying thief centuries ago. "Will you remember me . . .?" "Today, you will be with me. . . ." But they could just as easily have been spoken to you or to me or to the people who will see if we as preachers have some word of hope for them next Sunday.

I know the dangers of this approach to biblical exegesis. "Turn the students loose, and you will come up with all kinds of interpretations!" I believe I also know the possibilities of what can happen when a preacher approaches the text as if the electricity is still on and we are dealing with a live wire. The distance between then and now is collapsed, and we speak as if God is still moving and the word from God is as much for us now as it was for those who first heard it.

The Bible as Revealing God

The Bible is the source of controversy among some major religious denominations. Questions of interpretation arise. For example, should women be excluded from the ordained ministry simply on the basis of gender? Should gay and lesbian persons be permitted to occupy positions of leadership in the church? These and other issues have divided entire religious groups even as all sides have invoked interpretation of Scripture to support their sides.

Yet there is another issue some churches face. What is our basic view of the Bible? Do we see it as an inerrant book for all areas of life? For instance, do we take certain stories such as the creation account in Genesis 1 literally, or do we say it is a story whose purpose is to contend that behind all creation there is the creative, caring God? As believers in the truth of the Bible, are we to affirm every detail of the Bible, or are we to see the God whose image is reflected in the cultural and thought patterns of a certain segment of time? For some people, these may seem to be inconsequential issues, but for those of us in certain Christian traditions, these kinds of questions have divided us and wounded numerous people in the process. In my own denomination a person must affirm belief in the inerrancy or infallibility of Scripture in order to hold a position in the denominational bureaucracy or to teach in a convention-funded seminary. The contention of the conservative faction is that those of us who don't use words such as inerrancy simply do not believe the Bible is the Word of God.

While I believe that the motivation of certain leaders among the conservatives is more about power than protection of the Bible, I do want to say a positive word about a "high view" of the authority of Scripture. In teaching homiletics, I try to put heavy emphasis on the Bible as the source of the sermon. In my opinion, there is no other kind of preaching other than biblical preaching. Where I differ from those who advocate inerrancy is in how I view the intention of the Bible. In my opinion, it is not and was never intended to be a book of science, geography, or precise historiography. Rather, the Bible is a book of theology. More specifically, it is a variety of writings whose cumulative purpose is to reveal a God who is passionately committed to creation and who makes that loving commitment most fully known in the person of Jesus Christ. In the words of Paul, God is seeking to reconcile us to God's self. God wants to be known and opens grace to us in ways that expose God to our acceptance or rejection.

Frankly, this view of Scripture as revealing God makes preaching from the Bible more exciting for me. For one thing, it allows me to enter the various literature of the Bible with more appreciation. Those who know anything about the Hebrew psyché realize that the Hebrews were impressive tellers of stories. Their stories had a purpose. They were told to reveal something about Yahweh or to give us insights into ourselves, the world around us, why we act as we do, and why we sometimes resist the overtures of the divine. These stories penetrate deeply. As human beings, we are called to be stewards of creation. What kinds of stewards are we? We are called to be our brother's and sister's keepers. What about our brother or sister in Honduras, Guatemala, Iraq, or Indonesia? We are called to see God as the one who brings order out of chaos and purpose out of confusion.

What in our preaching today presents a God who is big enough to bring order in both our private and public worlds?

I contend that this arguing about inerrancy or infallibility has caused us to "flatten out" the Bible and to turn it into a series of propositions. The test of our faith then becomes our cognitive assent to these propositions. What about our relationship to God and to others? Isn't the fundamental call of the Bible a call to faith, a faith that beckons us to a relationship with God and to a risky "yes" to a discipleship where we are given no maps for the journey? Jesus asked those unlikely initial candidates for inclusion in his disciple band to follow him. Jesus didn't ask them to give mental assent to a creed about who he was. Jesus turned faith into an active verb. This is the exciting part. Fishermen such as Simon and Andrew left the things around which they had centered their lives in order to make the young Galilean preacher the new center. Did they understand all of who Jesus was? Could they articulate an airtight set of propositions about this God in Christ? Of course not. Faith was an adventure where ordinary people with all of their mix of faith and doubt dared to set out on a new course.

Something of this relational power needs to be rediscovered in the proclamation of the church. Think what many people in churches have become. For them, faith is largely a passive thing. They believe in certain ideas. Ask them what faith is, and they will likely tell what they believe. In many places worship is boring. The preacher repeats the expected platitudes, but we leave with no more dynamic sense of God than we had when we came. As a minister, I bear part of the responsibility. When have I preached as if everything was at stake? When have I dared to call others and myself into that risky relationship with a God who calls us into the not yet with little more than the promise of divine presence?

Frankly, it is easier to flatten out the Bible and to reduce it to a set of stiff doctrines to which we simply say yes or no. But think of what we miss! Before I was married, I believed in the institution of marriage. I even thought I knew what made a good marriage. You should see the sermons I preached before I was married. You talk about believing the right stuff—I believed it. I believed in the institution of the family before I had children. You guessed it. I have wonderful sermons on the right way to raise children—all preached before Laura Beth and David were born.

I have been married for thirty-one years. I have two grown children. My sermons on marriage and the family have a new ring of humility. I have learned I didn't know as much as I thought. Yet, think about what I would have missed if I had spent my life only believing in these things but never saying "I do" or never saying yes to a child whom I could hold and rock and to whom I could sing silly songs. Think of the laughter and tears I would have missed. Think of the piano recitals, the Saturday morning soccer games, the voice of a daughter, "Dad, I want you to meet him. I love him." It's called relationship. You and I don't just believe it. We live into and out of it. We experience it.

Isn't that what we are all looking for when we come to the place of worship? We want to experience the Holy One, to "know" God in the way that the Bible speaks of knowing God. Simply being told more about God does little if anything to help us to experience the intimacy of the God who journeys with us. The early church referred to Jesus as "the Way." The church itself became known as people of the Way. The enemies of faith first called the believers "Christians," and applying this noun to a dynamic movement may have been the most serious blow struck against this emerging faith. Nouns always go hand in hand with institutionalism, and the "people of the Way" soon were spending their time erecting structures and creating dogmas to support the "Way."

Understand that I am not against beliefs. A relationship such as marriage needs some beliefs to help support it. For instance, I need to believe in commitment. What I am against is the substitution of those beliefs for the experience itself. Unless I am badly mistaken, people today are hungry to know God. Many of them need to know that God believes in them as much as they need to believe in God. This means that people want to experience the biblical stories as their own. They want us to preach a God who is alive and at work, a God who makes God's self known and who journeys with us through the ups and downs of our lives.

When you and I read the Bible, we are amazed at how seriously time and history are taken. God comes into the ordinary time of people and transforms it into sacred time. God takes people and uses them to preach the need for justice in unjust times. God takes a stammering sheepherder on the backside of Midian, and Moses announces to the power structure of his day, "Let my people go." To a young woman not even married, God comes into the history of her life, and for all of her days and nights, she is left to "ponder these things in her heart." What we do not have in the Bible is a God who comes in a package of propositions that then have to be deciphered by systematic theologians. This is the God who acts, who reveals, who challenges, and who calls.

When I was younger, I used to try to imagine what God looked like. I always imagined God as "He" because that's all I heard. But the intriguing thing is that I always pictured God as extremely old and most of the time sitting down in a big chair. In fact, whenever God stood up, it took Him awhile to get His footing, and then He always walked with the slow gait of a very old person. I have nothing against old people. I am a card-carrying member of AARP. I sit more myself these days, and sometimes I have to wait for my legs to catch up with where my mind wants to go. But the real question for me is, why didn't I imagine God as more robust, more attractive, and more involved? Why was God always sitting when the God of Scripture is on the move calling creation back to its intended purpose? Why didn't I picture God as protecting the poor, comforting the bereaved, and calling any who would listen to be "people of the way." I read the words, but missed the big story. God comes to us; we come to God. This truth is the ultimate intimacy that gives life its deepest meaning.

The Bible That Interprets Us

Those of us who preach quickly become familiar with the task of exegesis. We open the Bible in our study. In front of us sits our text for

Sunday. Our task is to interpret, to allow the words to speak to those who will be listening. It would be much easier if we could say, "The Bible says what it means and means what it says." The Bible does have some distance to it, however. Written in other times and spoken out of the framework of other worldviews, the preacher's task is to try to reenter that world while making the message that is spoken relevant to his world. This always raises questions of subjectivity. We need to recognize that the work of interpretation is not an objective, exact science. All of us come to the Bible with traditions that have shaped us. When I drive to Baptist Seminary each morning to teach, I pass countless churches and a variety of denominations. If interpreting the Bible were a precise science, would all of these different churches claim to be proclaiming the Word of God? Therefore, when we speak, we need to avoid the sharp edge that comes when we believe we have a corner on the truth.

In order to preach, we do interpret the Bible. But what about the Bible's interpreting us? Preaching that is based on interpreting the Bible usually exhibits several characteristics. It is often doctrinal in content and argumentative in strategy. This kind of preaching seeks to convert the mind to a certain way of thinking. Before I take issue with this approach, let me say a word in its defense. This type of preaching is trying to say something important. It recognizes that many of us who come to church are ignorant of some of the fundamental tenets of our faith. That's important because we are talking about the beliefs that translate into the way we see and do life. We are not talking about being given a written exam or being able to name the first apostles of Jesus or being able to recite the books of the Hebrew Bible in the correct order. The fact is, none of that information may transform us. However, when we become aware of the grace of God and begin to live out of that knowing, that knowledge is transformative. The Bible seems to attempt to transform us. We are told about God but not in a way that simply informs us about the attributes of God. Rather, we see God as God seeks to encounter us and to transform us as we understand who we are and our need for the divine.

Connecting with the Bible

This is what I mean by the Bible's interpreting us. W. H. Auden, the famous writer of another day, frequently asked people if they had been read by any good books lately. We might ask the same question of ourselves when we read the Bible. Probably, all of us have had the experience of reading a book and being so caught up in it that we found ourselves identifying with the characters and experiencing for ourselves the story that we first thought was about someone else. We moved from being just a reader of the book to a participant in the unraveling of the plot. When we finally finished the story, we may have said, "I'm different because I have been read by this book."

In preparation for a sermon, the desire of a preacher is to enter a text so that it is not just exegeted but also experienced. This means that we have to live with the text, read it again and again, and hopefully the words we read become the words that read us. This type of preparation requires a sense of wonder and imagination on the preacher's part. To enter a text with only an analytical mind is to reduce the text to a manageable size. We do our word studies, read commentaries, and then report our conclusions to the congregation. The problem is, we never allow ourselves to be engaged by the text and to experience its life. Our sermons are often spoken dispassionately because nothing life-changing has gripped us or transformed us. We speak the words of the sermon, but they lack the conviction and resonance that come from a firsthand encounter with the biblical text.

When we don't enter into the text and become a part of its life, we usually wind up with a lot of distance between ourselves and the words of the Scripture. We have studied the text, but we have not permitted the text to intersect our being so that we speak of things that are fresh and real to us.

Several years ago our family was in the "station wagon" stage of our lives. As we planned our summer vacation, I suggested that we go to Miami, Florida. I grew up in Miami. "I'll take you to all the neat places that meant so much to me. We'll go to the ball field. I'll show you the church where I came to faith. We'll go the old neighborhood, and I'll even buy you a vanilla coke at Breeding's Drugstore." For some reason, cokes with vanilla syrup were big in my high school days. "In fact," I told my family, "I'll even take you to Miami High School and show you where Miss Tourtellot taught me Latin for three years." By this time, my family looked absolutely bored. For some reason, it's hard to communicate excitement if you haven't "been there and done that."

My family knew how important this trip had become to me, however. "Dad's going through a life change. One of the symptoms is nostalgia. We'll humor him through it." So we loaded the station wagon and headed south. I hadn't been to Miami for awhile. The roads have changed, the buildings are gone, and big new structures have taken their place. Was I ever lost! After an afternoon searching in the hot sun, we finally found the high school. "Dad," my daughter said, "can't we go to the mall?" "Sure," I replied, "this should take only a few more hours." "The motel has a nice swimming pool," my son reminded me. "The water will still be there," I said. "This is the high school," I proudly announced, as I lined up my family for just a few more pictures.

Of course, I realize the building held no memories for any of them. They were good sports to indulge their dad. For me, however, the memories were wonderful, especially of Miss Tourtellot. I thought she was about 95 years old when she taught me, but, of course, I thought all my teachers were 95. She wore big clunky shoes. When the bell rang for class, Miss Tourtellot yanked the door shut, and for an hour there was nothing but Latin. My teacher wasn't big on small talk. We never asked what she did for fun. We just assumed she did Latin all the time. I heard people say, "Latin is a dead language." These people never encountered Miss Tourtellot. She never met a Latin pronoun or verb she didn't like. The Caesars were her personal friends, or at least it appeared that way to the students. Not only did she teach Latin; she *was* Latin. As students, we couldn't separate the subject from the teacher. What passion she had, and she was equally passionate that we both learn and love Latin. She was the first teacher to call me "Mr. Bugg." "Mr. Bugg," she said, "you did your translation last night, didn't you?" "Yes, ma'am," I squeaked. "Then," she said, "you tell the class everything about that verb on line 3."

If I was correct, I was greeted by Miss Tourtellot's same stern face. I never remember her saying, "That's good." I just wiped the perspiration off my face and hands and thanked God it was over. But if I made a mistake, I knew from the furrowed brow and the scowl on her face that I had injured her and the whole Roman Empire at the same time. I heard about it, too. "You did your translation, Mr. Bugg. Apparently, not well enough. Tomorrow we will see if you can get it right." Maybe I was a little masochistic to endure three years of Latin, but in a strange way, I loved my teacher. Latin was so important to her. She taught with a passion. She was engaged by the subject and expected us to share her passion and engagement.

It's been many years now since I sat in Miss Tourtellot's class. It seems like such a long time ago (come to think of it, it is). To this day, though, I can still conjugate the verb "to be" in Latin and recite certain pronouns. Granted, there's not a great market for that skill, but I think about what I've forgotten from other subjects or maybe what I never really learned in the first place. What I remember most, however, was my teacher. She was in love with Latin, and in a strange way, those of us who were her students felt the contagion of her passion.

Those of us who preach are, of course, talking about things far more consequential than Latin. We are talking about God. We are speaking about the One sent from God who changes our lives and gives us new direction. As preachers, we sit in front of the biblical text so that we can experience its life-changing impact. We then go to the pulpit with both information we have learned about the text and with the transformative experience of having been encountered by the words.

Not long ago I preached a sermon from the story of Simeon and the infant Jesus in the Temple. Luke 2 records this encounter of Simeon with the baby and his parents. I knew certain facts from previous study. This was an expected trip to the Temple. As Jewish parents, Mary and Joseph knew that Jesus needed to be circumcised and consecrated, and Mary needed to undergo the ritual cleansing. I also knew that one of Luke's favorite techniques was the use of "contrast." Old Simeon meets young Jesus. In the first chapter of

Luke, old Elizabeth expecting her first child is visited by her young relative Mary who also is expecting her first child. The woman who waited years to hear, "You're having a baby," greets anther woman who never expected to hear, "You're having a baby." Luke is a master preacher, and one of his favorite techniques is contrast.

As I sat alone with the biblical text, Luke 2:25-35, reading it aloud again and again, I became fascinated with the words of Simeon's song. In Latin, as the ghost of Miss Tourtellot would remind us, the song is called the "*nunc dimittis*." With the baby in his arms, Simeon sings to Jesus, "For my eyes have seen your salvation, which you have prepared in the sight of all people, a light for revelation to the Gentiles and for glory to your people Israel."

This is a prominent theme in Luke's Gospel. Jesus comes for both Gentile and Jew. Simeon is saying this baby will embody the encompassing love of God, a love that will break down all barriers of exclusion. We know from Luke that one of the biggest divisions was between Gentiles and Jews. Luke's second volume, the book of Acts, pivots on a council in Jerusalem where reluctant converts such as Simon Peter finally recognize that the move to faith isn't "Gentile-Jew-Christian" but simply "Gentile-Christian." For the first-century church, this was a remarkable, revolutionary decision. It changed the whole face of missions. Everyone could know personally the God revealed in Jesus Christ.

Yet I have a problem as I prepare to preach. I am preaching to a congregation that doesn't feel the "Jewish-Gentile tension." It's going to be very difficult to get them to experience the revolutionary impact of these words. They will agree that this was a first-century division, but to the church where I'm preaching, the result of the Jerusalem Council is assumed. When this church talks about missions, it speaks about the gospel for everyone. I doubt that anyone to whom I'm speaking will disagree with Simeon that Jesus is "a light for revelation to the Gentiles and for glory to your people Israel." What I have on my hands is a solution without a felt need. For me to talk about how revolutionary this word is, will be to miss the "isness" of my situation.

I'm preaching to folks who are already in the choir and converted to Simeon's song.

We still have the issue of inclusion. Simeon is singing about a Savior for every person. Imagine with me what that may mean for today. Let's assume that many folks who come to hear about God's gift of life really feel they don't deserve it. In fact, most of us may feel that way at times. Who am I to be included in those whom God loves and wants to embrace? Think of those to whom we preach. Some of them have been wounded deeply. Their problem isn't arrogant pride that shakes its fist in the face of God and screams, "I don't need the gift." Many of us know we need the gift. What we don't know is that we deserve it.

Probably every Sunday that you and I preach there are those listening to us who carry the terror of having been abused as children by adults whom they trusted. At the time in their lives when they should have been developing a sense of trust out of which they could live, these people were robbed of the gift. Some have learned to disguise the pain. They wear nice clothes, live in fine neighborhoods, and seem to us to be attractive and at ease. But we don't know the anxiety. We don't understand as we speak about trust in God why these folks do not seem to understand. Perhaps if we put ourselves in their places for a minute, we could better relate to their feelings of isolation. We can appear to be on the inside of everything but spend all of our days and nights feeling like the outsider. We can belong to the right groups, the right clubs, the right sorority or fraternity but never really feel we belong to anything except our deepest fear of being abandoned.

Simeon was singing about inclusion. In the first century inclusion concerned your status as a Gentile or Jew—whether or not you belonged to God. It meant that whatever your heritage was, you had a shared hope. The barriers had come down. The walls were broken. God had come for everyone. Am I stretching the biblical text by preaching that it means everyone? Can I name some of the barriers that keep us from being reconciled to God and to others? May I let the text interpret who we are as listeners? Will the Word have meaning on an Advent Sunday when I stand to preach about the song that an old man Simeon once sang about a baby who one day would speak of a God who includes all of us, even those of us who think we do not deserve it?

Certainly, this use of the biblical text has risk, but I want to take it. To me, the greater risk is to preach words that have no connection to the hearers. Those of us who preach always need the humility of knowing that we sit before the Bible and that its truths are more than we can encompass with our minds or envelop in our words. We will exegete the biblical text, and the text will exegete us. We will place the words in their historical context, but the words won't be pinned down to one place and one time. The words keep bounding into our beings, sometimes challenging and sometimes comforting. They are words that have life to them. In fact, we even dare to say that if we listen carefully to the words, we may hear the Word itself. When that happens, not only do the words have life, but we also have life.

Questions for Reflection

1. Why is the Bible the source of our preaching? How would you describe your view of the Bible and why the Bible has unique authority?
2. Think of a biblical text that reflects the worldview of its time. How would you interpret the message for our day? What would you say to a listener who heard your sermon and responded, "If you change one part of the Bible's message, what prevents you from changing all of it?"
3. Pick a biblical text that reveals something important to you about God. How does the text reveal that? Does the text give you a new image of God? How would you communicate that image to the people listening to your sermon?

Quickening

Luke 1:39-45
Sandra Hack Polaski

I expect it will be happening for me just about any day now. When it does happen, I don't know what words I'll find appropriate to describe it. Different women speak of it so differently: a fluttering, a thump, like plunging downhill on a roller coaster. One woman told me, "If it feels like you've got a frog down there, then you'll know it's the baby."

It's an occurrence that is often still called by its old-fashioned name, "quickening," that experience sometime during the second trimester when the expectant mother first is able to feel the movement of the child in her womb. And there's a sense in which it is the remarkable, almost magical moment when the expectation of this child suddenly becomes *real.*

I suppose my concept of pregnancy prior to now had all come from that mental image of the woman late in pregnancy, waddling around with a belly out to here. One of the things that has taken me by surprise is how unreal a pregnancy can seem for the first several months. Oh, sure, I've had many of the classic pregnancy symptoms: I've felt queasy and tired, but somehow that didn't really make me feel *pregnant.* And even though my pregnancy was confirmed, early on, by the most up-to-date, gee-whiz technologies, somehow it has been hard to connect, in my mind, the fuzzy picture on the ultrasound screen with the realization that a new, separate human being is taking shape inside my body. And so now I eagerly await the moment I know is soon to come, when, finally, I will feel that movement within me, and then, in a remarkable new way, I will know that this is real, that this is for sure.

It happened just that way, it seems, for Elizabeth. Poor old Elizabeth, postmenopausal Elizabeth, whose husband Zechariah had seen an angel who gave him a message that took his breath away—more than that, took his whole voice away. And Elizabeth conceived a child—she knew she had conceived, knew this fatigue was more than just advancing age, knew that the way she felt in the morning wasn't just what she had eaten the night before. But it all still felt so unreal, in a way, so unbelievable, as she waited and wondered through those first long months.

And then, one day she heard a familiar, beloved voice at the door. It was her young relative Mary. And just as suddenly she felt the flutter, the thump, the kick. Mary was there with amazing, exciting news, and Elizabeth had amazing, exciting news of her own. In that moment it all became real to her—Mary's presence, her message, and the reality of the child springing to life in her own old body. She cried out in joy—what else could she do?—and embraced young Mary with a benediction that fit them both: "Blessed is she who believed that there would be a fulfillment of what was spoken to her by the Lord." Blessed, indeed; not just Mary, who would go on to sing a beautiful song of praise, but also and especially Elizabeth, who in that splendid moment found the certainty, the confirmation, the reality of the promise she had already received, but that until now had seemed so unreal and hard to believe. The fulfillment—ah, yes!—the fulfillment of the promise was on its way, just as the Lord had spoken, and now she knew.

What is quickening within you this Advent season? What flutters in your stomach, sends you on a wild ride, kicks you in the ribs, and demands your attention? What job lies in your future? What worthwhile project has captured your imagination and will not let you go?

Perhaps you have known your calling a long time, lived with it many months and years, so that you have known seasons in which it seemed very far-off and unreal. You have trudged through your studies, lived in student apartments, worked part-time jobs, and pinched pennies while your friends launched careers and got promotions. You've had your calling confirmed, of course, by all the gee-whiz technologies: Your Myers-Briggs is exactly suited to the sort of ministry you plan to do; your ministry profile confirms your gifts and strengths. You know that tug at your heartstrings isn't just sentimentality, but genuine compassion and concern for people in need. But it seems so long to wait. This isn't how you had imagined ministry, and preparation for ministry, would be. And there are times it is so hard to imagine, so hard to believe.

And then, like Elizabeth, you hear the message, you hear the good news, you hear the proclamation of the Messiah who is to come. It's hard to explain the feeling exactly, but it's more than just a sensation or an emotion. Now you know. Now it is real. Now the fulfillment is on its way. Not that you have achieved everything it takes to prepare you for ministry. Oh, no; still more waiting and preparation lie ahead, not to mention plenty of hard labor. Or, like me, you may still be waiting for it to become real to you. You know that it is there, that it is within you. But this Advent season finds you waiting, anticipating, listening for the proclamation of the good news that will quicken within you that which you have nurtured so long.

Do not be afraid. Wait in hope, for the fulfillment *is* on the way. As surely as the child of Bethlehem is the promised one sent by God, so is God's calling to you about to come forth. As the first Christians heard the words of the prophet as a message directly to them, so we, too, hear them today: "Unto *us* a child is born." What quickens within you when you hear the good news, the gospel of Jesus the Christ? Rejoice, for God's promise to us is surely being fulfilled. Amen.

Chapter 5

Releasing the Message

As we preach, you and I discover that there are three main questions we ask ourselves in the preaching event. The first question is, "What will I say?" Obviously, this is a fundamental step. The preacher encounters a biblical text. With the awareness of her listeners in mind, she fashions a focus or a point for the sermon. "What one main thing will I attempt to communicate in this message?" she asks. This means that an effective preacher has to learn to say "no" or "later" to other parts of the text that are appealing. This is difficult, especially for the imaginative proclaimer. This preacher sees much in a biblical passage and is tempted to want to give voice to all of the insights. The discipline of proclamation demands that we wait to talk about some things so we can give sufficient time and attention to the development of our primary focus.

After arriving at what we believe we want to say, we then turn to the commentaries, dictionaries, and other tools that will shed light on the pericope and the point we have chosen. Once in a while we will modify the focus of our sermon or even change it completely as we read what others have to say about the selected passage. It may become clear to us that what we are trying to say cannot be supported by the biblical text. However, I caution against abandoning ideas too quickly.

Not every preachable thought has been published in someone's commentary, and the preacher who knows his audience may find in his own journey with the text a message that connects with the people who will hear the sermon. Believing that a text has a present and a past, I find it difficult to be arbitrary about precise rules that can always determine whether a passage of Scripture is being used correctly. Because of this uncertainty, I prefer to encourage the imagination of preachers rather than to turn the whole exegetical task into a rigid process whose main intent is to find the "right meaning"— whatever that may be.

I also recommend staying with the original focus from the text for a more practical reason. When we as preachers find something in a biblical passage that excites us, we enter the process of preparing the sermon with great enthusiasm. Often, however, as we prepare the sermon, we move through times when some of that enthusiasm diminishes. After all, the preparation of a sermon is a labor, even if it is a labor of love. When we encounter times when fashioning the sermon seems more work than love, what do we do? Sometimes we abandon our original idea for the sermon and go in search of something else to say. At times this may be necessary, but often it lengthens the sermon preparation process and pushes the preacher into the eleventh hour still searching for the one point to preach.

The fact is that most of us as ministers have a certain amount of time in which to prepare a sermon. If we have a need to feel excited about everything we are going to say or to create the "perfect" sermon each time we peach, we are in deep trouble. We spend too much time scrambling around for just the right thought, and, therefore, we sacrifice time we need to absorb the sermon once we have completed its preparation.

After deciding what we will say, we then turn to the question, "How will I say it?" That is, what plan do I have to communicate my message? What strategy, form, or design will I use to put my words together so that they will be heard by my listeners?

I suggest three things that need to be considered as the minister shapes a sermon. First, what forms or designs are congenial to the minister's own personality or gifts? This doesn't mean that preachers should not work on expanding their repertoire of ways to present a sermon. I grew up in a preaching culture that emphasized only one form—the deductive sermon that usually fell into three points. As far as I knew, that was the only style that existed. I heard some ministers who incorporated entertaining stories into their messages, but these stories were usually interpreted as a way to reinforce a point of the sermon. Therefore, I have been greatly indebted to homiliticians who have introduced me to inductive and narrative preaching. In fact, one of the most important new books in homiletics, *Patterns of Preaching: A Sermon Sampler* (ed. Ronald J. Allen, Boston: Cowley Press, 1998), introduces us to a variety of sermon types or forms and includes sample sermons illustrating each type.

One fundamental factor often has been omitted in the discussion of sermonic forms, however, and that is, "Can the preacher do it?" That is, do the personality and gifts of a minister permit him or her to roam at will in this suddenly expanding sea of sermon shapes. This issue was focused for me several years ago. A preacher was having difficulty in his church. The congregants were complaining about his sermons. "All he does is tell stories," some of them said. Others remarked that the stories seemed unrelated. "We don't know what he's talking about," some of the folks responded. "Besides, he tells a lot of the same stories, and they weren't that good the first time."

I had been asked by the pastor and the church to analyze his preaching. He had the misfortune to follow a highly deductive, straightforward preacher who thought stories were ornamentation and who used them only in the service of a point in the sermon. As the new pastor and I worked together, I asked him one day, "Who is your homiletical hero?" "Fred Craddock," he replied without hesitation. "I heard him speak at a conference one time, and I've read a couple of his books," this minister continued. "Dr. Craddock tells wonderful stories, and I want to be just like him."

Maybe we were dealing with a church that wouldn't have liked even Fred Craddock, although I seriously doubt it. "Good choice," I told this minister. Craddock is among my favorites, too. But I had a minister beside me who was about to lose his job even as he tried to imitate one of the best in the business. After listening to several tapes of this minister's sermons, I concluded that it is probably not a good idea to mold ourselves after any preacher no matter how good he or she is. Second, I'm not sure this minister had the gifts to be the kind of inductive, storytelling preacher that Craddock exemplifies. I saw a more linear-thinking person next to me. When we read several biblical texts, and I asked him to talk about them, he usually gave me what he thought the point of the text was. While his insights were excellent, he had little comment on characters in a narrative text and talked little about the "feel" of the passage. Maybe some of these qualities could be developed, but he wasn't there yet. His stories were too long, too detailed, and too convoluted. There was nothing to stitch the sermon together into a meaningful pattern. Apparently, this minister had not read or understood the stress that Fred Craddock puts on "unity" as an essential ingredient in a sermon.

All of this is to say that those of us who preach have strengths, and we have limits—or as some of my students call them, "growing edges." We have a certain personality, a certain timbre to our voices, a certain way we present ourselves, and certain ways of thinking and feeling. All of these influence both what we say and the way we say it. Again, while we need to stretch and improve the ways we communicate, we don't want to spend our days ashamed that we can't seem to preach like someone else. We claim the gifts we have, and we try to become the most effective communicators we can.

In addition to our personality and the boundaries we all have, a second factor in the way we preach is the biblical text itself. One of the most exciting developments in the preaching art has been a renewed emphasis upon the form of a biblical text. Previously, preaching had been so set on finding the point of the passage that it had often disregarded the literary structure and the context of the passage. Listen to preaching in predominantly white churches. We are discovering what our African-American sisters and brothers have known for years. Retelling a biblical passage in an alive and imaginative way can be a powerful way to communicate not only a message, but also the texture of a biblical text. The form of a passage of scripture is like the tune of a song. The words of "Amazing Grace" are moving even when they are recited, but when combined with the familiar tune, those words are capable of taking all of us back to the time and place when the grace of God became amazing for us.

A third factor in the way we preach is the listeners. To whom are we speaking? What is important to them? How are they used to hearing a message? What are the ways that will communicate to them? These are all important but difficult questions to answer precisely. Some homiliticians say that we can only speak in imaginative, evocative ways. Some suggest that we are dealing with a generational issue. Those who have been raised in a television culture want picturesque language and quick-changing images, whereas their grandparents want more concrete language and sermons that have well-defined points.

While age, background, education, ethnicity, cultural differences, and a variety of other factors affect the ways we listen, we need to be careful about overgeneralizing on the way people listen. For example, I once was pastor of a church located next to a university. Many of the faculty and administrators were members of this church. The worship style was very formal. The church had a succession of ministers who were highly educated and tended to be more cognitive and intellectual in their preaching styles. The problem was that the students at the university were not attending the church. They were going to other congregations in the community that felt more "like home." When I talked to the students on campus, they said things such as, "First Baptist is just an extension of the university. We listen to lectures all week. On Sundays we want something that sounds more like a sermon."

Churches located near universities often make a false assumption. They assume that students want worship and preaching that stresses intellectual stimulation and mirrors the same issues and styles with which the students deal Monday through Friday. As the new preacher, I had to make some tough decisions. Should we ignore the needs of the students, even though our church was within walking distance of the campus? Should we continue to strive for intellectual stimulation and then criticize the students for wanting something other than just more mental challenge? Should we try to preserve the intellectual integrity of the church's worship while at the same time doing things that may make our services warmer and the sermons more appealing to the heart and mind?

We did make some changes. In shaping the sermons I tried to be sensitive to proclamation that had some fiber in the content but also had some evocative and emotive qualities to it. Our church managed to make it through the changes with a minimum of difficulties, while also attracting a much larger number of students to our services. A few faculty members grumbled that we were prostituting worship by modifying some choices in music and some subjects for preaching, but by and large we made it through without hitting any major icebergs.

My point is not that I had the answers to worship or preaching that always connects. Frankly, I have serious problems with a church's worship that is shaped strictly by market analysis. Those persons who raised questions about change in our university context were a good corrective to the idea that we simply preach in a way that draws the largest crowd. As we made the changes in that church, the staff, leadership, and I were careful to try to preserve the intellectual integrity of our faith and to make modifications grounded in what we thought was a solid theological framework. While I believe that what we did was successful and not too radical, I still review the decisions we made and certainly can argue the other side.

What I am concerned about, however, is the listener and finding ways to get the message heard. We ministers are trained in theology. Like students in law school or medical school, we have our own vocabulary. We learn ways of looking at the Bible that most laypersons don't know. In the lounges of theological seminaries you will find students talking about "redaction criticism," but if these students take this important tool and lay it on the churches where they serve, they will be met by bewilderment. "So that's what they are teaching you at that seminary. We thought you were studying the Bible."

Where are our listeners? I'm convinced we needed to make some changes at the university church where I was pastor because we had missed the students. They really didn't want the sermon to be a lecture. Once in a while they wanted to sing a hymn they had sung at their churches back home. While we want people to grow in their understanding of their faith, we can become arrogant when we see ourselves so far ahead or think that everyone else must rise to our level. We quickly destroy intimacy in preaching if we give people the impression that we have a corner on what is right or appropriate, and other folks are ignorant if they don't share our point of view.

Release

The preacher asks, "What do I want to say?" Then she asks, "What way do I say it?" The third question is, "How do I speak it?" The

126

sermon is not a paper whose purpose is to be read. That may be a secondary benefit, but we are not preparing sermons that are so involved and intricate that people will have to buy our books if they want to understand what we first tried to say to them. Preaching should be an oral experience. We are talking about a well-prepared message that is spoken in a way people understand and that moves them closer to God.

I have chosen the word "release" to describe what traditionally has been called "sermon delivery." I'm not altogether satisfied with the term "release," but it helps to convey the idea that the preacher "experiences" the message as he prepares and then the sermon comes through him in a way that communicates intimacy and authenticity. *Passion* A large part of my concern is the recovery of passion in the preaching event. Again, some of us come from traditions where a word such as "passion" has unfortunate overtones. To some of us, it may conjure up images of someone who displays all types of emotions or tries to manipulate the hearer's emotions while not saying anything that seems to be even the least prepared. I have seen preachers laugh and cry while some in the congregation have said, "That's passion."

We as preachers sincerely believe that what we speak in a sermon is of tremendous consequence both to us and to our listeners. In a world that desperately needs direction and where many seem to be searching for spiritual moorings, I'm convinced that people will not hear us if we read sermons or speak words in a way that communicates we are not intimately invested in the message. That doesn't mean we have to scream, cry, laugh, or throw a fit. But it does mean that our voices and presence share the deep importance of what we say.

Interestingly, we have often separated the preparation and the "delivery" of the sermon. For many years John Broadus' book, *On the Preparation and Delivery of Sermons,* was the primary textbook used in the field of preaching. The title communicates this unfortunate bifurcation. I contend that preparation to speak and speaking itself are inextricably linked. From the outset we prepare to say something from God through ourselves to others. That recognition affects all of the preparation of the sermon and keeps us focused on the end of the process—as preachers, we are called to proclaim.

Remember, there is no magic bullet to achieve authenticity or to create intimacy. In fact, trying too hard to achieve this may mitigate against the very thing we are trying to do. In the most profound sense, qualities such as intimacy and authenticity are not learned in the same way as grammar or mathematics. Rather, these qualities are byproducts of our believing in the God about whom we preach, believing that our words can be used to make a difference, and believing in ourselves that each of us has something to give.

Receiving Ourselves

Most of us have been told more than once in our lives, "Be yourself." The difficulty is when we don't believe "ourselves" to be adequate in a certain situation. Public speaking is a frightening event for many folks. A recent survey showed that speaking in front of others was the greatest fear people have. Therefore, those of us who teach preaching have a special stewardship. Some who sit in our classes have dreaded the introductory preaching class more than any other course in the curriculum. Like most theological schools, we require our students to preach and then to be evaluated by their peers and professor. The tables get turned whenever I speak in the campus chapel. It's amazing how many students love to offer their critiques. I guess that's a price you pay for being presumptuous enough to teach preaching.

I realize that students come to a preaching class with different levels of potential. I'm convinced that we can all become better in our communication, but I also know there are intrinsic qualities all of us have that significantly determine the outer limits of our development. As a teacher, I see myself trying to do two things. First, I want each student to stretch himself and to be as good as he can be. I begin the semester by pointing out the obvious. Even though I teach proclamation, I can improve and do it better. I never want to stop growing, and these students will be both my learners and teachers.

The second thing I try to do is to get students to believe in themselves and to recognize that they can communicate publicly better than they ever imagined. Nothing gives me more satisfaction than to see a student grow in her confidence to articulate the faith. Not all of our students will be parish preachers. While I am committed to the preparation of people to serve in the church, I recognize there are different rooms in God's vocational house. In fact, one of my most pleasing experiences was having a student who was passionately committed to inner-city ministry. He was deeply concerned about the poor, the homeless, and the marginalized. This compassionate young minister wanted a "hands-on" kind of ministry with these people.

I'll never forget the day Jon preached in class. We were all genuinely moved. It was beyond just the "good sermon." Talk about passion. A minister who was connected to people connected us to a biblical text, and those of us who listened remembered again the concern of Jesus for the "least of these." After class that day I talked with my student who had become my teacher. "Jon," I said, "I'm not in the business of telling students what to do with their lives. In fact, I want you to follow your vision. But along with that, I want you to believe that you have the gift of speaking to people who have resources. You are able to move people. Have you thought about continuing to cultivate this gift of preaching? Somebody like you can be an attractive advocate for those whose voices may never be heard in the gated comminutes of our city's suburbs." For me, this was a sacred moment. I saw the butterfly emerging. If I'm not badly mistaken, I see in Jon a minister who for years to come will remind all of us that God has a special affinity for those who often get left behind.

In teaching preaching we are disseminating important information. No one should exit the class without learning ways to put a sermon together, but more than that, as teachers, we are in the business of confirming gifts God has given and instilling confidence in all of us who realize that preaching is a daunting challenge. Some of my students tremble when they come to preach. I no longer tremble. I wonder why. Is it because I'm so good that I no longer need to tremble? Is it because I've done it so often that I know how to camouflage the exterior signs of fear? Or is it because I sometimes forget how critical preaching can be in the shaping of lives, and I see what I do as just part of the rhythm of my life? I fear taking preaching for granted. I fear that one day it will be just something I do. When my students' hands tremble, they remind me that I need to tremble more.

I so much want for myself and those whom I teach to accept their gifts. I want them to be the best they can be, but I don't want them to try to be anyone else. We have voices and gifts from God. We have personal histories filled with pain and pleasure. We have faith histories where we have lived in the fresh breeze of the Spirit, but we have experienced the dark nights of the soul. We have encountered God and been encountered by grace. We have so much to say. Only we can say it. If we don't, the story from our unique perspective will never be heard.

This doesn't mean that we don't learn from others and improve the areas in which our preaching may need help. For example, those of us who may not be as adept at telling stories can learn by listening again and again to the techniques of effective storytellers. Those who may have problems in the "pace" of their sermons can profit from preachers who know how to use pauses and who know when to slow down in order to allow something that is said to sink in more deeply. In teaching I have found this particularly important in the transitions that mark changes in the movement of a sermon. While we have encouraged our students not to structure all of their messages with, "My first point is . . ., My second point is . . ., we have not always done a good job in giving them alternatives. Effective use of pauses, some slowing of the rate of speech, and the employment of questions that have a repetitive effect all may be ways to make transitions. For example, "Why? Why does Jesus say that to this woman? Why does the man who held the children and touched the leper suddenly tell Mary, 'Don't hold onto me'? Why?"

While we learn from others, we want to avoid trying to duplicate the style and presence of someone else. Not only is it a denial of our own giftedness as a child of God, but also it appears disingenuous and greatly hurts our authenticity.

Getting Inside the Message

All preachers face the question, "Whose message are we preaching?" By that, I don't mean taking someone else's sermon and speaking it as our own. We are all influenced by the ideas of others. No sermon I have preached has been completely my own in the sense that every notion and every phrase originated with me. I imagine that's true with every preacher. I'm indebted to countless people who have taught me both by what they have preached and the way they have preached.

When I talk about whose message we're preaching, I'm speaking more about the issue that the apostle Paul surfaces. Paul professes that he does not preach himself but rather Jesus Christ. The apostle wants his listeners to understand that his message comes out of his experience with Jesus Christ and is preached to call and to encourage others in that experience. Paul seems clearly committed to a message whose focus is Jesus, who he is, and what this Jesus the Christ can do to transform the lives of people. Whatever disagreements we may have about some of Paul's emphases such as his hierarchical approach to family life or to ecclesiastical life, it is hard to argue with the man's passion. As Paul testifies, his message is from Jesus Christ and focuses on Jesus Christ.

Yet, if Paul's letters are any indication of his preaching, his proclamation bears a certain "Pauline style." Paul is not like "every other preacher." He doesn't proclaim Jesus by simply repeating Jesus' name. Obviously, the message of the one who changed him has come through this disciple of the Damascus Road, and the message bears his imprint. For example, certain issues are often fashioned in response to a particular church situation, but the theology itself seems to be embedded in the Apostle's bones.

Writing to the Philippians, Paul wants these folks whom he loves to understand what the presence of Jesus can mean in the shifting circumstances of their lives. "For to me to live is Christ and to die is gain." Those are the words of someone whom Jesus the Christ has changed and who has found an extraordinary power for life. In this sense, the answer to the question, "Whose message is it?" has to be

131

both God's and Paul's. The proclamation doesn't come to us directly from beyond. A human being has experienced something profoundly meaningful and now comes to say, "This is one of the things that faith means to me. Whatever happens, know this: "For to me to live is Christ and to die is gain.""

Not only substantively but also stylistically, the message has the handprints of Paul. Paul is the master of the argument. His sentences seem interminably long. He is deductive in his style. Paul utilizes rhetorical devices such as repetition and appeal to memory. Again, both the message and the means of communication are inspired but have the marks of the man all over them.

In preaching, this awareness is important. Those who preach don't preach some pure, pristine, untouched message that then becomes like "every other sermon we have heard." Part of the exegetical process is personal. We do not hold the biblical text at arm's length and handle it as something we never engage. In fact, we are called to engage the Word of God and to be engaged by God. We are called to enter the biblical text so that we can feel it, touch it, taste it, and most of all experience it. We encounter God, and then we have to decide if Paul was right in saying, "For to me to live is Christ and to die is gain."

This process of "internalizing" is critical to the release of the sermon. We can't release something that has not become a part of our beings. A word of caution needs to be said. This "internalizing" does not mean that we have appropriated for ourselves all of the truths of Scripture, and, thus, we preach only what we've experienced. To say the least, that is presumptuous. I may affirm with Paul that "to live is Christ and to die is gain," but I will spend all of my days struggling to receive the depth of that truth and to incorporate its assurance into the bloodstream of my being. All of us have heard preachers who seemed to speak as if they constantly lived in the glow of Easter Sunday. Their sermons are filled with words of victory over every problem with which most of us struggle. When you and I listen to these preachers, we get the impression that there is nothing in the Bible that is beyond them, and the despair, the doubt, the pain, and the anxiety that most people experience have been eliminated in their existence.

While we listen to these types of sermons and wish that faith were this simple, we know it's not true. Life has struggles. Even Paul writes about those times when he was caught between opposite feelings, disparate desires, and longings that seemed at odds with each other. When we preach as if coming to God suddenly makes life carefree, we lose much of our audience. They know that's not true. They are being downsized in their businesses, getting divorces, and have children who are on drugs. The people who listen to us need to know that we understand the life in Christ is not perennial springtime.

Therefore, when I talk about "internalizing" the text, I'm not speaking about adopting a kind cheshire cat smile that seems oblivious to the complexities of life. At times we will preach about things in the Bible that have been stitched into the fabric of our lives. Other times we will read the word from God, point to the mountain, and invite people to join us on the journey. The important issue is that we have entered the text in such a way that it becomes both the message from God and the message from us. I see no way to separate ourselves as preachers from what is preached. What is in the Bible is a message for us. We are the recipients of the life-changing words, and we preach as persons who are invested in the wonder of this good news. We are not dispensing a prescription designed only for others. This is our medicine, our message; this is meaning for our own lives. We don't deliver goods prepared by others. We release from ourselves the things that are nourishing our spirits and the things we want to nourish us even more.

This view of preaching makes it impossible to separate preparation from the "delivery" of the sermon. As we enter imaginatively into a biblical text, our bodies become a part of the process. Preparation of a sermon is not just an exercise of the mind. What does my face look like? God says, "Abraham, here's the test. Take your son, your only son, the son whom you love. Take Isaac to the mountain in Moriah and offer him to me. " When I read those words, my eyes are wide in wonder. I'm awestruck. My face is already reflecting what I hope later will be seen in the preaching event. This is powerful stuff. It's hard to preach this text without appropriate effect. Yet some of us have raced through these words as if we were giving the weather report on a perfectly normal day.

What about the rate of our delivery? Again, we enter and experience the text. God issues an incredible demand. Do the words slip glibly out of God's mouth? Does God have any idea what God is asking? Surely God does. The writer stresses, "your son, your only son, the son whom you love." God knew how desperately Sarah and Abraham had wanted a child. Isaac was the fulfillment of a longing and the assurance of a future. Isaac was the laughter of parents who never expected to laugh like this. Yet God asks for Sarah's child: "Abraham, take him to the region of Moriah." I preached on this text in a church and wondered out loud, "Where was Sarah when all of this was happening?" After the service a mother in the church that day met me at the door. "I know where Sarah was. She had climbed the mountain before Isaac and Abraham, and behind every thicket, she had placed a ram to be sacrificed in the place of her son." Not bad. I realize this isn't in the Bible, but this was a mother speaking to me about what she would have done if she had been Isaac's mother.

So we preach on this text in Genesis. Do we speak the words from God to Abraham in a matter-of-fact way? Do we race through the words without feeling that somehow we are learning something life-changing about a man, a woman, a child, and their God? "Take your son," God says, "your only son, the son whom you love." God seems to be lingering with each phase as if they all reinforce the enormity of what God is asking. God could have said, "Here's the test. Abraham take Isaac." Rather, it is "your son, your only son, the son whom you love." If we have internalized the depth of that demand, we will never be able to rush through it. We will speak it as the sacred moment that it is. God comes to ask what God wants. All belongs to God. Yet, in this moment, Isaac is not laughter for his aged parents. He is pain and heartbreak, and the cost of obedience to God seems too great a price to pay.

What about gestures? When I first started preaching, I would practice my gestures. On the door of my seminary office, I have a copy of a Kudzu cartoon. The Reverend Will B. Dunn has videotaped one of his sermons. He watches himself in slow motion. "I love," the Reverend says, "to watch myself in some of my finest moments." What a comedy that must have been as I delighted in some of my best moves in front of the bathroom mirror. Like a choreographer, I worked to put the movements to the words. I could hardly wait to have a chance to preach and show my latest sweeping gesture. As I recall, not only was my gesturing too stylized, but also I had a bad sense of timing. My gestures and words were off a split second because I was concentrating so hard on what I would say next and what movement would accompany the words. If you've ever seen a minister whose message and movements are even slightly out of sync, you know how silly that looks.

The gestures need to rise from the preacher's experience with the text. What is the text saying, and what is it doing? "Go to Ninevah," God says to Jonah. We have tension and struggle. Our hands can reflect that resistance. The nation of Israel, represented in Jonah, seems caught between the altruistic desire to share the blessing received from God and the selfish impulse to keep Yahweh for itself. That struggle intensifies when the call to bless others is a call to those who have abused Israel. Why give the good news to the Ninevites? What have they ever done except trample us under their feet? Jonah does have a point in waving off the will of his God. Everything about Jonah reflects resistance as he boards the ship for what he considers a more deserving audience.

Yet, Yahweh is relentless in compassion. We are talking about expansive gestures. Israel's God wants to be every person's God. "Why do you curse the vine's withering, Jonah, when there are 120,000 in Ninevah who belong to me," God says. Jonah is closed up within himself, arms wrapped around his own prejudices. On the other side God extends the reach of compassion and embraces all God has created.

So many aspects of releasing the message depend upon our getting inside of what we are saying. As a minister prepares, he feels what he will say, and already his body begins to reflect what he will speak. Resistance, openness, fear, love, inclusion, exclusion—all of these and a thousand other experiences become internalized in the preacher, and then when the sermon is spoken, it is released and not just delivered.

Seeing the Listeners as Friends

Viewing listeners as friends is one of the most important but often overlooked dimensions of the preaching event. As preachers, we are speaking words, but we are speaking those words to persons. In most places those people are diverse. Some diversity is more obvious to us. We see women and men, children and adults, black and white, and a myriad of other obvious differences. Other differences are more subtle. If we are the pastor of a church, for example, we learn that people listen in different ways. Some like their sermons streamlined and straightforward. Other folks like more ruffles and flourishes.

We may learn other differences. Some people listen to us with trust and openness, while others are more cynical and skeptical. Some listeners reflect their responses to what we say with animated, alive faces. With others, it is a guessing game for the preacher. We can't tell from their expressions whether the sermon is being heard or whether our preaching is connecting with them. One of the worst things we can do is to assume that because we don't see any overt response, we are not liked. Some folks simply have a difficult time expressing themselves. Among some people there is a fear about letting other people know what they are feeling. Therefore, we as preachers need to be careful when we conclude that someone does not like what we are doing. The fact is, with some people we may never know.

I remember vividly an experience I had when I resigned as pastor of a church. There was a man in the congregation who had never said the first positive word to me. When I preached, I thought he looked distracted or bored. I would have told you, "If there's anybody in this church who won't miss me, it will be this man." When I resigned, he wrote me one of the most meaningful letters I've ever received. He recalled specific things I had said. Frankly, I was shocked.

I suppose I recall that incident because it had a nice ending. Obviously, there are other folks to whom I have preached, and I've heard nothing. That's probably one of the most difficult things about ministry. We enter ministry with a sincere desire to make a difference in people's lives. The reality is that sometimes we don't and other times we may never know if we have made a difference. We offer the gift, but ultimately we trust God to use our offering.

In a sermon we do preach to people. How do we see these people? Do we see them as our enemies? If we do, that leads to a style of speaking the word that sounds adversarial. When we speak about issues such as trust and compassion, we speak with an edge to our voices that belies our message and undercuts our authenticty. This is not a call for the minister to be naïve. If we have been at ministry for any length of time, we know that some people in churches operate out of their agendas for power, and we know our own needs to control or to get approval. Yet, if we allow these things to affect our basic approach to people, we will become curdled with cynicism and a victim of our distrust.

Listen to the way some ministers talk to people. They belittle the congregation, undercut the church's confidence, and generally give the impression that they are the only adult in the room. I'm well aware of ministers who have been deeply wounded by the actions of their churches, but I'm also aware there are churches that have been hurt by preachers who have ventilated their hostility and used the pulpit as a weapon to hurt and not a place to bring healing.

Not long ago I talked by telephone with a recent graduate of our seminary. He has been called as pastor to a church in a small North Carolina town. We talked about what it's like to go from the seminary to be the pastor of a church where you have the regular rhythm of preaching. He told me about how he prepared his sermons and how he was working to deliver them more effectively. What I recall most from our conversation, however, is what he said about the church where he serves. "I couldn't be happier. These people have loved my wife and me and have shown their care in so many ways."

"I couldn't be happier," this young minister told me. I know what you may be thinking. Give him a few more years. Give him some more deacons' meetings, and a few more business meetings where he is criticized, and he will be singing a more cynical song. I really hope not. I know he's just in the first inning of the ballgame. Not every pitch he throws will be a strike. He'll probably walk a few batters and give up some hits. Some people in the stands may think it's time to bring in a new pitcher. But my prayer for my former student is the prayer I have for me and for every other preacher I know. When we stop caring for people and lose our basic trust in the church, we have lost all hope for intimacy. It's difficult to convey care to people you really don't like.

Do you know what I try to assume when I preach? Sometimes it's hard, but I'm trying to do this more. I assume that the people sitting in front of me want to hear what I'm going to say. When I do that, my speaking is so much more natural, and I don't have to think about doing outlandish things to get people to listen. Recently I heard about a minister who seemed to take forever to get into his Sunday sermon. When I preach at a church where I've never been, I usually take a moment to express my appreciation for the invitation. If the pastor is someone whose ministry I know, I will say some affirming words about the person. Even those of us who are guests, while wanting to be warm and grateful, have to watch that we don't go on forever and delay the sermon too long.

The minister about whom I heard was the pastor of the church. Yet he seemed to feel the need to tell jokes, make announcements, and express profuse thanks to almost everyone who had participated in some way in the worship service. The congregation was becoming frustrated. Was their minister not prepared? Was he anxious and, therefore, he did all he could to delay the moment of truth? His jokes were usually the "old saw" variety, the ones that have been around the block so often that they really need to be put to rest. When this minister finally began the sermon, he often rambled and seldom finished by noon, an imperative for most of us in the white church tradition

While there were obvious problems in his preparation, there were also serious concerns evident in his speaking. First, he reflected a lack of discipline. People want to know that their minister is prepared when she speaks. They don't want the structure of the sermon completed as the preacher is standing still trying to bring order out of chaos. We can't release something that really isn't ours. We discipline ourselves so that we can move through the sequences of preparation and allow ourselves enough time to live into the message. We may decide to change some things as we speak, but we certainly don't want to be "inventing" the sermon as the congregation watches us experiment with first one approach and then another.

A second factor that may have contributed to this mister's pre-sermon monologue was a feeling that his congregation was really not on his side, and the people hadn't come to church because they wanted to hear what he had to say. If this is our attitude, we may spend excessive amounts of time trying to be cute and clever and make people like us. Sadly, this usually has the opposite effect. People become irritated when we spend too much time trying to tune the violin. They want us to play music, and they don't want the concert to go overtime because we were so late getting started.

This matter of time is a factor for most of us who speak. There may be a few churches where the preacher can go on and on, but most of us preach to listeners whose outside limit is about twenty to twenty-five minutes. Here, I'm speaking from my tradition where the sermon is still a central component in corporate worship. In other traditions where there are more acts of liturgy or where the serving of the Lord's Supper is the focus, the time for preaching may be less. As a minister, I assume the listeners are my friends. However, I don't want to presume on that friendship by turning the preaching moment into a congregational endurance test.

Staying Focused on the Message

Releasing a sermon assumes that we have a message to release. We try to say something well. In fact, we believe we speak about the most crucial aspects of life. As Christian ministers, our message is that God's love has embraced us in a variety of ways but most fully and completely in the person of Jesus Christ. While we recognize pain and suffering, we also speak about a transforming hope. We preach a Lord who died, was raised, and is now living. We proclaim that this risen Christ lives in us, empowering us to be different and to make a difference in a world that God loves. The qualities for which people seem to be searching are a part of our proclamation—salvation, peace, joy, hope, faith, love—this is the preacher's vocabulary, and we preach to ourselves and to others about a God who changes lives.

We deal with vital issues. Yet we preach to many people who seem increasingly disinterested in the God about whom we speak. They want qualities such as love and peace. A lot of folks talk about finding joy, but there doesn't seem to be much interest in being committed to follow Jesus Christ. Bookstore shelves are replete with writers who offer their own paths to fulfillment and who tell us how we can possess peace and prosperity. Sanctity and success are presented as two sides of the same spiritual coin.

Trying to remain faithful to our calling as preachers is a challenge. While our task is to speak to people about how they can possess peace and find stability in the storms that come, we know that to be faithful in our proclamation we must preach the cost of discipleship. We can become discouraged when we believe our message isn't wanted or being heard. Over the years of our preaching, that discouragement erodes our passion. One Sunday we find ourselves standing in the pulpit speaking the right words but feeling disconnected to the message or even to the God about whom we speak. The issue is how to keep our passion in the proclamation event.

For those of us who teach homiletics, it's not enough for us to prepare students by giving them a few helps to sharpen their craft but not to prepare them for a lifetime of ministry. Hopefully, we are preparing preachers who for most of their lifetimes will make their way to a place where they will speak the words of life. It's not enough to say simply gesture like this or remember to make eye contact with your listeners. These are ministers who will discover that their vocation is demanding, and there will be days when they will preach in pain. They may continue to gesture and make eye contact, but the sadness is when they have lost their own touch with the deepest things.

How can we release something that has long since lost its meaning for us? No matter how sharp our speaking skills are, people will sense when our spirits are running on empty. Perhaps, even more sadly, we will sense it. Then, the choice becomes either to leave the pulpit or to stay and simply go through the motions of ministry hoping that somehow we can make it to the end.

For those of us who preach, I don't know anything more important than to stay in touch with the message that once set us on the way. Someplace, somewhere, somehow, those of us who speak were touched by the God of grace, and we came to know that grace through Jesus Christ.

Recently my daughter was home. Laura Beth is married and is a doctoral student a Harvard Divinity School. She wants to teach religion. I look at her and have enormous pride in what she wants to do, but mostly I'm proud of the wonderful young woman she's become. Dads are allowed to call their children "wonderful." One night as she and I were sitting together in the family room at our house, she turned to me and said, "Dad, I love you." That night I had tears in my eyes when I went to bed. I recalled how quickly a little girl had grown up to become a woman. I remembered vacations our family had taken. I thought about bedtime stories and the nights I had tucked my children into bed. They would say, "Daddy, I love you." Years have passed, and now I'm Dad instead of Daddy. But the "I love you" is the same, and it still deeply moves me. Have I outgrown the need for love? The answer is no. That message, "I love you," means as much to me today as it has on any day of my life.

I know there are Sundays when ministers come to preach, and we don't "feel" God as intensely as other times. Sometimes we don't even "feel" like preaching. But we remind ourselves of our message. The people in front of us need to know that God loves them. The choir members behind us need to know that God loves them. As proclaimers, we need to know. So we listen as we speak and release a message that is deeper than how we may feel about it that day.

Gardner Taylor was right when he observed, "Preaching is a presumptuous business." None of us is adequate for it, yet we keep coming to preach. The people are waiting. They want to know if we have anything to say to them. "God loves you," we say, and on some days we feel it so powerfully that we must say it. Who knows? In the process both preacher and congregation may be changed. Who knows what God may release and which of us will be set free? Therefore, let's preach!

Questions for Reflection

1. When you preach, are you more concerned about communicating a message or getting the message you have prepared spoken as precisely as you have written it?

2. How do you see yourself as a preacher? Do you believe you have something worthwhile to say? Do you find yourself continually trying to emulate someone whom you consider to be a good preacher?

3. How do you view your listeners? Do you believe they need to hear what you are saying? Does it bother you if someone gives you no indication that he or she is listening?

Sermon

007s of the Faith

John 20:19-23
Blythe Taylor

Around the nation this month, churches and educational institutions find themselves in the celebrative throes of commencement exercises. That adrenaline-surging, high-anxiety occasion that brings both hopes and questions galore. That day, when we realize in a palpable way that a chapter is closing in our lives. Commencement by definition is a beginning. Just as the previous chapter closes, so must a new one begin. Today, we celebrate the accomplishments of those who are graduating from educational institutions.

Today, universally, the church also celebrates another commencement exercise. Remembering that fear-filled day in the upper room when Jesus, after his death and resurrection, appeared to the disciples and breathed upon them that they might receive the Holy Spirit. Today, we celebrate Pentecost.

Pentecost was the Greek name for the Jewish Feast of Weeks that occurred fifty days after the Passover festival. It was originally an agricultural feast that celebrated the end of the grain harvest. By the time Jesus arrives in the upper room, he has already appeared to Mary Magdalene. He has told her that he will soon ascend to his Father in heaven. Mary has notified the disciples of what she has seen. Then we hear these words:

> When it was evening on that day, the first day of the week, and the doors of the house where the disciples had met were locked for fear of the Jews, Jesus came and stood among them and said, "Peace be with you." After he said this, he showed them his hands and his side. Then the disciples rejoiced when they saw the Lord. Jesus said to them again, "Peace be with you. As the Father has sent me, so I send you." When he had said this, he breathed on them and said to them, "Receive the Holy Spirit. If you forgive the sins of any, they are forgiven them; if you retain the sins of any, they are retained."

Can you see them? Probably remaining in the upper room where they had eaten their last supper with Jesus, the disciples sit on pins and needles. The door to the room is locked. Still in shock over Jesus' death, those who are present sit in silence, fearful that if they make a sound, the Jewish leaders will also arrest them. What has kept them in this room? Maybe their fear? Maybe the memories of Jesus? Maybe the suggestions they've heard, like Mary's, that he is alive? Whatever the reason, they find themselves twiddling their thumbs, wondering what they are going to do now. They might well feel the same anxiety that comes with commencement.

Suddenly, out of nowhere, it seems, there appears this figure that looks like Jesus. I imagine that each person in the room must have sat there for a minute trying to figure out if this image was real or some sort of hallucination. There they sit, looking around at each other's facial expressions trying to determine if anyone else might have seen what they think they saw. And then, making matters more confused, the image says, "Peace be with you."

The greeting is an everyday salutation and yet also a customary blessing offered almost as a prayer. No doubt when Jesus says it, it is loaded with meaning the disciples just don't get. Surely, in disbelief, the disciples turn away to gain perspective before they look again or wipe their eyes in hopes of gaining clarity. It is then that they all see the nail-pierced hands and his wounded side.

Seeing the scars on his body produces understanding for the disciples. It helps them to realize this image as the earthly Jesus, and understanding brings an overwhelming sense of joy and amazement.

Realizing that they didn't quite understand his earlier blessing, Jesus says again, "Peace be with you." This time, as William Barclay calls us to understand, they get it! They understand that Jesus is saying, "May God give you every good thing." Then Jesus proceeds to give them one of the greatest things. By breathing upon them, Jesus is able to give the gift of God's presence, the gift of the Holy Spirit.

The symbolic action of breathing upon them makes clear that the Spirit comes from Jesus following his ascension to heaven (Witherington.) That Spirit comes out of Jesus' very being. This is a crucial moment in the whole gospel. It is here that the Spirit will transform some apprehensive disciples into active leaders.

Usually we find that dark, handsome British gentleman galavanting around the world with beautiful women. All the while, he is fighting for right, fighting for truth. He is known by his *savoir-faire*—the cleverness that despite his mishaps with technological gadgets always leads him to a win. We know him by that deep voice and his trademark introduction, "Bond, James Bond." We know him as Agent 007. In every episode the opening scenes show evil running rampant in the world. The camera quickly arrives at the central headquarters with everyone abuzz about how to solve the problem at hand. The solution? To call for Agent 007. His success rate is unbelievable! And it is believed through his faithfulness that goodness will win this battle. And so he is sent to do the work that the agency director, because of his position, cannot do. James Bond has been commissioned to save the world.

In the same way, God has sent Jesus to the disciples as a delegate. Jesus is dependent on them as couriers to deliver his message to everyone, to be his agents of the faith. So he commissions them to save the world, saying, "As the Father has sent me, so I send you." In so doing, he is giving us what has often been called "the church's charter." This means that just as Jesus is dependent on his disciples, his church, to be the messengers, so the church is dependent upon him to be the message-giver, to give the credibility in a powerful way to the message, to be the place where we can turn in all times.

Jesus' sending out the church stands parallel to God's sending of Jesus. The relationship between God and Jesus is dependent upon Jesus' perfect obedience and perfect love. No less is expected of the church in its relationship to Jesus.

Jesus' action of breathing the Spirit upon the disciples is a creative one. He offers them new life . . . a new beginning, transformed from their fears to carry out Christ's tasks in the world. This is their chance to be the 007s of the faith. His blessing for them is that they go out as the church with the privilege of conveying the message of God's forgiveness to God's people. So, in the last verse we are told that this power to proclaim forgiveness comes connected to the power to warn others that forgiveness comes to those who repent. Jesus' purpose in his gift of the Holy Spirit is to ensure that his disciples form a family of forgiveness.

On this day we honor these graduates. We commission them to be couriers of God's forgiveness and God's presence. On this day we remember the gift of God's Holy Spirit. May we remember that we are disciples, agents of Christ. As such, our ultimate mission is to recognize the gift of God's presence as the beginning of life and to live each day in perfect love and obedience. As this day brings a new chapter to our lives, let us remember that all of us are called to be the 007s of the faith.

Completed
10-3-07